Confessions of an Outer Banks Filly

Memoirs of Sybil Austin Skakle

Cover photo: Sybil, around four years old. The orange in the crook of her arm seems more interesting to her than the goose she was asked to hold for the photograph.

ISBN Number   1-880849-37-2

Manufactured in the United States of America

To those who still call Hatteras home
and to those, alive and dead,
who were part of these memories

Foreword
The Austin Family and Makeup of Early Hatteras Community

*E*very two years since 1974, the descendants of Mogieannah Oden and William Wheeler Austin have assembled at Hatteras Island for a reunion celebration, spearheaded by Ruby Austin (Dalton Lee) Burrus, who maintains an updated family tree. At last count, there were over four hundred who are now part of its branches. They are people who were "born Austin, children of Austins, or someone married to one of them." I was born Austin.

Historically, the Austins have been on Hatteras Island a very long while, even before this first 1755 tax record:

Original T.O. 105—Taxables in Currituck, 1755: Thomas Austin -1, John Ballance -2, Austin Scarborough -1, Sarah Burrus -1, John Scarborough, Sr. -2, John Burrus -1, John Scarborough, Jr. -1, William Howard -1, George Scarborough -1, George Howard -1, Samuel Stow -4, Michael O'Neal -2, Thomas Robb -1, John O'Neal -2, Thomas Robb, Sr. -1.

The belief that Thomas Austin was the first Austin on the island is supported by the above and by grant records in the North Carolina Archives in Raleigh. In 1756, Thomas received "170 acres in Currituck County, Hatteras Banks, joining Sound at the mouth of the

Thorough Farr [probably thoroughfare] near his own line, the Sea Beach, and a point near the hills."[1]

In 1760, he received "144 acres in Currituck, Hatteras Banks, joining the plantation he now lives on and the sound."[2]

Early tax records list the amount of property owned by these named Austin: William, Cornelius, Thomas, Sr., Thomas, Jr., and Daniel, a single man.[3]

An early legal document indicates that Cornelius and Daniel were brothers. We assume they were sons of Thomas Austin, Sr.[4]

In the first U. S. Census, the following Austins are listed as heads of families: Thomas, William, Daniel and Thomas, Junior. Cornelius is not listed.[5]

Other family heads listed at that time are as follows: Ballance: Daniel, Jervan, John, Thomas, William, William (again) and Willis; Burris (note spelling): John; Quidley: Thomas and William; Stow (note spelling): Joseph and Samuel.

It is reasonable to suppose that Rolinson and others came later. But, the history of these first families probably goes back further than 1700. One Thomas Austin, a mercer (a seller of cloth) shipped from England around 1620. That is not to say he is the Thomas who became progenitor of those on Hatteras Island. He may have been. My father, Andrew S. Austin, used to say there were three Austin families. I suspect all descended from Thomas.

Inventory of an estate commenced in 1777 lists that inventories were proved in 1799 for Mary Bracham, indicating she has property from a decedent (person deceased), probably her husband.[6] There were blacks, probably brought there, and Indians who lived on Hatteras Island. Bracham may have been a Native American name. She may have been black.

A bit of later history—John Rollinson[7] wrote this note in his diary: "new Hatteras church commenced July 25, 1877 by I. A. Austin was finished February 7, 1880 by William B. Ballance and James A. Stow. Rev. George L. Fulcher preached the first sermon."[8]

Traveling in the United States and Europe, I have found Austins listed in telephone directories of many places, even Edinburgh, Scotland, and Brussels, Belgium. We are a prolific and mobile people.

The Hatteras Austin Family Tree was putting out branches long before John Oden, grandfather to Mogieannah, washed ashore. The Island was teeming with life, the sea with fish, and men were trying to get ashore by falling overboard, if we are to believe all we have heard.

—Sybil Austin Skakle

Chapter 1
Mama's Pianos

❧

*M*ama's first piano had its day in the upstairs living room of the house Daddy had built between 1916 and 1918. Before Ellsworth Burrus built Atlantic View Hotel—the only hotel Hatteras Village on the Outer Banks of North Carolina has ever had—people who came to stay overnight or longer used the upstairs living room where that piano resided. Many hands, skilled and otherwise, touched Mama's pianos over the years.

Mama told a piano story about a scary night she had before I was born. Daddy had gone to Elizabeth City on business. Mama, alone in the big house with three small children, heard a ghostly visitor playing the piano in the front living room, up the hall from their sleeping area.

Awakened by the sound of the piano, she lay in her bed afraid to move, listening for another note. Full of dread, she heard a note, a pause, then another, another, and then several in quick succession. Petrified by fright, she waited to hear footsteps or a creak of the wooden floor while she made plans to save her children and herself. Nothing! Finally, in the wee hours of the morning she fell into sound sleep.

Next morning she discovered cat paw prints on the piano keys and decided one of the children, on purpose or by accident, had allowed one of the stray cats hanging around the premises to slip inside. Finding evidence that the ghostly musician had been feline, she cared not how it got into the house or that it had.

Sales representatives called "drummers" visited various small businesses, Austin General Store one of them. Island isolation—no bridges then—required that they stay overnight. Maybe they tried Mama's piano.

General Billy Mitchell came to Hatteras in 1923 to do that offshore bombing that proved his theory that a ship could be sunk from the air. Some pictures owned by our family show soldiers, one of them a pilot named Charlie Austin, and planes brought there for that event. Perhaps some visited my family and maybe played Mama's piano.

Another picture shows an assembled crowd enjoying a picnic at Durant Lifesaving Station, September 5, 1923, the day of the bombing. People lined the walk going from the main building of Durant Lifesaving Station to the station kitchen. Though I had not yet been born, I loved to look at the picture and pick out people I recognized, especially Mama, brother Shank, and sisters Marjorie and Jo.

By 1930 some rich industrialists and professionals had discovered Hatteras Island. Finding it a sportsman's paradise due to its remoteness and exclusiveness, they came to hunt and fish. A colorful bunch, they stayed at our house before they built Gooseville Gun Club on the southern end of the Island.

Van Kampen Heilner of New York, my favorite, wrote articles for *Field and Stream* and paid attention to four-year-old Sybil Dean, admired my new dress, called it "gorgeous." I am told that I rebuked him, "It's not. It's pretty." He took my picture with one of the Canadian geese he had killed.

Albert Lyons of Detroit, inventor of the automobile bumper, was a handsome, amiable, white-haired, blue-eyed gentleman who made a generous gift of the Hatteras Girls Club building to the young women of the village. He hired a young, beautiful recreational director for its beginning operation. I learned my first tap dance step on a Saturday morning, thanks to Mr. Lyons, but I did not progress.

Henry Stellwagen of Philadelphia owned a company that manufactured roofing materials. And there was a Dr. Hand, who particularly loved to shoot the beautiful black and white geese. One evening at the dinner table, as we enjoyed eating one of those geese, he promised sister Marjorie to get her all the geese gizzards she could eat. We had visions of flying gizzards being shot out of the air. One of those guests or a friend they brought with them may have played Mama's piano.

One day I was on hand to witness the maneuver that brought that first piano downstairs. However, it is the piano that took its place that I knew best.

Daddy had gone to Elizabeth City to buy a new car. Mama decided she should have a new piano if he was buying a new car. A salesman appeared at the right time for Mama, wrong time for Daddy. But first she had to get that heavy instrument downstairs. I do not know if she traded it in on the new one or sold it to someone in the village.

Mama could move anything. When I was only a little girl, she recruited me to help her move the chicken house. She was indomitable. With broom handles and rugs we once moved the old kerosene refrigerator, which never did well, it seemed to me. We took down bedsteads and transported mattresses from room to room. Mama, not having a budget for redecorating, moved furniture to change things a bit. Daddy used to joke that he had to be sure to turn on the light before he tried to get in bed at night.

Mama had to recruit some strong men from customers or loiters around the store to move that piano. Determined, she may have recruited them from village men passing by on the dirt road in front of our home. She found them, and the arduous task of bringing the heavy, bulky piano down the hall to the back of the house and down the inside stairs began.

The railing at the back of that hall that protected us from falling down the stairwell had to be taken down. (It was never as solidly founded again.) Slowly, painfully, the old piano was inched and guided down that dark, inner stairway to our downstairs living room. No longer a guest upstairs, the piano became part of our daily lives. While it was often moved from place to place in the living room, it remained in the living room downstairs for as long as it survived. It was the focal point for much that went on under our roof and in our lives.

Before 1936, Dr. Edouard Lippé, who taught Nelson Eddy voice lessons in New York City, stayed and played Mama's piano. The most colorful person who ever did, he usually came with a male companion; and if my memory is correct, he stayed all one summer and on into the fall at our house. Another summer he rented a house.

A short man with dark eyes and hair and a handsome face, Lippé had a body that had been misshapen by a motorcycle accident, making his imitation of a chimpanzee all the more vivid and believable, a chimpanzee that played Mama's piano.

One year, another voice student, with a name that sounded like Kovach came with him. The looks of the big, blond Polish or Nordic giant were in total contrast to Lippé himself. They weathered one hurricane with us, helping keep up our spirits with music. That may have been 1933. It could not have been in '36, because Mama did not mention them in an account she wrote of that year.

When Nelson Eddy got called to Hollywood, he soon had Lippé join him. On their way to Oakland, California, to visit Mama's brother, Uncle Caswell, Daddy, Mama, and four relatives visited Lippé, Ryland, and another gentleman at their residence in Hollywood in July of 1936. Mama was thrilled to shake hands with Dick Powell.

Dr. Lippé referred to Mona and me as "The Little Darlings." My sister Jo thinks it was in derision. It may have been. But he sent me his picture from Hollywood and gave me a book on zoology. Was he trying to influence a child to be a scientist? Well, I became a pharmacist!

I enjoyed the delightful man he was. His attention to me was impersonal. Maybe he had never been around children before he came to stay with us and play Mama's piano.

Mama spent many happy hours, as well as difficult ones, playing and singing. Music expressed her joys and soothed her sorrows. She wanted her children to have the pleasure of playing. So each of us was exposed to piano training, more or less.

Margie, the oldest sister, probably had the best training and the longest. Corlette Burrus, son of the man who built the hotel and provided the first movies to local folks, taught her. She played more difficult pieces than I could ever master.

Jo, my sister five years older, had two teachers, Addie Ghoul and Rev. Bell, our Methodist minister. She believed Bell to be the better teacher.

Even Shank, ten years older than I, did the beginners book. However, I never remember that he competed for the piano.

Mama traded Eula Williams, a Wanchese lady, room and board for music lessons for Mona, four years younger, and me. I had learned the keyboard very early and had formed terrible fingering patterns before Eula came onto the scene.

Mona liked to say that she never learned very much because she could never get to the piano. True, maybe, with four others to vie for our turn—Mama, Margie, Jo, and me.

Our home was home for many others through the years. Besides Eula, Clyde Talent, a high school science teacher from the North Carolina mountains—Franklin, specifically—stayed for two years. Margaret Morris of Spartanburg—near Erie, Pennsylvania—stayed three years and taught English and literature. Ruby and Shank were married and lived at our house for a while. Mona and I may have been the only two at home the year Mama filled all the rooms with teachers.

Anderson Midgette, later well-known Hatteras Island real estate man, came from Rodanthe, and stayed for two years, 1939 and 1940. Before consolidation of the schools, he chose Hatteras over Manteo and stayed to graduate.

Clyde Talent fell in love with a local girl, Anita Willis, whom he took back to his mountains to live before the war began in 1941, deserting the sand fiddlers. He teasingly declared me a sand fiddler and taught me to play Set Back. He died during the conflict.

Margaret Morris went back to her family's chicken farm in Spartanburg, Pennsylvania, to teach and take advanced courses in library science. All my efforts at matchmaking failed. Christ was her first love. She went to a movie with a fellow from the weather bureau once. The boys kidded her in school the next day. She never went again. Neither she nor her two sisters ever married.

However, without any help or encouragement from me, Anderson married one of our high school teachers, Kathryn Hurdle from Elizabeth City, and fathered five beautiful daughters. But my story is pianos.

Well, we only had heat in the downstairs living room and one bath, located at the top of the stairs. An early stove burned coal, brought to Hatteras on a barge. A dirty fuel, it was stored in a coal bin to the left of the back door and brought into the house in a coal bucket. A kerosene heater warmed the bathroom while heating water in the tall tank in the corner behind it. We lighted the oil heater in the upstairs living room for special occasions. Once the family photograph album got burned up in that stove. Shank had hidden it supposedly to keep Mama from showing off his baby pictures. Generally, however, everyone assembled in the downstairs living room on cold evenings, except Anderson.

One evening, I sat at the piano playing "What a Friend We Have in Jesus," by the see-the-note, play-the-key method. Suddenly Mr. Talent, who sat grading eighth grade science papers, sprang from his chair and rushed up the stairs. I never doubted that I had thoroughly unnerved him and never again practiced in his presence.

Mama and Daddy must have become immune or had learned the art of tuning out when we practiced. Fourth in line, I knew Mama to be happy when we tried. Most of the time, Daddy was in the store attached to our living quarters. When he was in his chair reading the newspaper or a book, I never remember him telling me to stop playing. I marvel at their patience, their tolerance.

If Mama's piano could have talked, if it had gray matter, a brain to record the events it observed, it would have had a lot to tell. Many hands had played it or abused it. Children with sticky fingers as well as accomplished musicians had explored its treble and bass keys to coax sounds from it. With our parents having four daughters and one son, the house was a hub of activity. Friends and family were in for short visits or extended stays. It might have told about the hurricane when the tide threatened to invade and rust its strings. And about the strong men who lifted it, wooden drink crate by wooden crate, until it reached the ceiling, to keep the tide from ruining it. How Margie played its keys even then to see how it sounded in the air.

While the Hatteras Fire Department was still many years in the future, that piano survived a fire. Mama, cleaning the wooden floor— no longer covered with linoleum—with gasoline, thought she had turned off the oil heater that had replaced the coal burning one of earlier years. Suddenly, the living room exploded into flames. Her visiting brother, Commander George Daniels of the U. S. Navy, saved the day. When all the extinguishers that could be found were used or failed, he directed anyone in the store at the time to grab flour sacks and Arm and Hammer Baking Soda to empty the containers on the fire to smother the blaze. Smoldering upholstered furniture was hauled to The Slash, a body of water running through the village, to be dumped to extinguish the fire. Only the piano survived. Daddy cleaned and refinished it and the piano stool to look better than before. Having graduated from Hatteras High School in 1943 and being in college, I missed that excitement.

That piano could have told you about a little girl who used to play the pictures on the sheet music she found in the piano stool, before she could read the notes or the words. It would tell about how her tears wet its keys when she was disappointed in love as a teenager. Not once, but many times. It would recall how that girl struggled to learn to play the sheet music she acquired for herself whenever she went to Norfolk, Virginia, Elizabeth City, North Carolina, and once to Baltimore, Maryland. It would remember how she leafed through hymnals to learn music of faith from those who shared their feelings, insights, and theology by writing the lyrics and musical scores that she loved.

When her mama died, that little girl, grown up with children of her own, found playing the old piano painful. It recalled the hours she and her mama had sat side by side on the old piano bench to sing and play hymns. More tears wet the keys of the old piano that once belonged to her mama.

By 1969 the old piano, still looking good, had rusted strings, a sounding board too brittle to hold a tune, and a key or two that did not sound. Persons living in the house wanted the space it used. They discarded the old piano. Only the piano bench remains, having an honored place with the girl who loves her memories of Mama's pianos.

This piece has appeared previously in *The Island Breeze.*

Chapter 2
An Eventful Year

❧

Nineteen thirty-six was an eventful year for our family. On January 10th, the morning of my tenth birthday, I was excited and joyful, anticipating something special to be in the wind because I had a birthday. Instead, before Mona and I got out of our bedroom, behind Mama and Daddy's, Mama came in and said, "I'm glad you're happy, Sybil. I hate to tell you that your brother Shanklin was stabbed last night in Buxton. The wound came so close to his heart that he is fortunate to be alive."

That news made me feel guilty for being happy and dashed my hopes for any sort of celebration. I could not be happy with my brother in the hospital where he had been flown while I slept. However, childlike, I am sure I resented that he had to get stabbed the night before my tenth birthday.

He had been at a place known as the Bucket of Blood. Even before this incident, fights were frequent between the young men who went there to drink and dance. Fellows in the CCC camp at Buxton and perhaps some from the WPA camp in Trent (Frisco) hung out there, as well as the local youth. Some supposed it might have been one of them who wielded the knife. His attacker was never identified. No arrest was made, since all we had was a magistrate, Dr. H. W. Kenfield. Just how much authority that may have given him and if it included making arrests, I do not know.

While Shank was at the hospital, they discovered he had a stomach ulcer, a fortunate discovery. Mama began to puree everything he ate, forcing it through a metal colander. Gerber's Baby Food Company, if it existed then, did not have baby food on store shelves at Hatteras.

Certainly I cannot remember how the day went after that. Perhaps Mama and Daddy drove to the hospital to be with Shank. If so, someone, probably family, would have been requested to stay with the rest of us. Margie at eighteen would have been away at school. She finished high school at Peace College in Raleigh, and the following year she went to Greensboro to take a one-year commercial course at Woman's College of the University of North Carolina. She had been home that summer, but not on January 10th.

On a much happier note, on July 4th, Mama and Daddy, with four of Mama's relatives from Wanchese, started across country in a four-door sedan—before air-conditioning—to make a surprise visit to Mama's and Aunt Lillian's brother Cas and his family in Oakland, California. Mama's journal told about their adventures and vicissitudes. Oil had to be changed every one thousand miles, and they had to buy a tire or tires along the way. One night they slept on the desert. They had one blanket among the crew. Mama made comparisons between the scenes they saw and those back home; a wheat field and the ocean were both beautiful to her eyes. Names they saw on billboards and businesses indigenous to Dare County intrigued her.

Mona and I stayed with off-the-island relatives. Margie, Jo, and Shanklin were at home. Grandpa Wheeler had been asked to stay with them. After the first night, he left. He went home to where he lived with his youngest son Horton and his family, who had small children. Andrew's adult children were too noisy for his liking.

In California, the travelers made a visit to Eduardo Lippé in Hollywood. After they arrived at the Daniels' home in Oakland, Daddy went back to spend more time with his old friend while others stayed to enjoy family. Mama was thrilled to have an opportunity to shake hands with Dick Powell, a favorite movie star of hers, before they left Hollywood. At the beginning of his career, Powell sang a lot while Ruby Keeler danced. He had become a voice student of Dr. Lippé's.

September, 1936, brought one of the worst hurricanes we had known to our coast. There had been many hurricanes in my lifetime before the one of 1936. One in 1933 had been very bad. Others, occurring long before I was born, are documented. Copied from The National Archives, Record Group #27, a letter dated August 21, 1899, tells about a hurricane that swept over the area 16th, 17th, and 18th of August. The writer, S. L. Dosher, Hatteras Weather Bureau Observer, gives his personal account of his experience at Hatteras. Writing to the Chief of Weather Bureau, U. S. Department of Agriculture, Dosher says he talked with people who could remember back 75 years, who said the storm of 1899 was the worst they had ever known.

"During the early morning of the 17th, the wind increased to a hurricane and at about 4 AM it was blowing at the rate of 70 miles; at 10 AM it had increased to 84 miles, and at 1 PM it was blowing a velocity of 93 miles, with occasional extreme velocities of 120 to 140 miles per hour. The record of wind from about 1 PM was lost, but it is estimated that the wind blew with even greater force from about 3 PM to 7 PM, and it is believed that between those hours it reached a regular velocity of at least 100 miles per hour. The barometer began falling rapidly about 8 AM on the 17th, and by 8 PM on that date it reached the unprecedentely low reading of 28, where it remained for about an hour..."

Mr. Dosher's nine-page letter tells of his personal efforts to reach the Hatteras Weather Station, sometimes finding the water to his chest. He gave a lengthy description of the damage, which he estimated to be $16,000 to $20,000 in Hatteras alone in 1899 dollars!

However, the one in 1933 —before hurricanes had names—frightened me most. It had no parallel in my memory. In more recent years, there have been more devastating ones to Hatteras Island. However, it is that one I remember best.

Wind was gusting up to 100 mph, taking railing and chimney off the Weather Bureau, which we could see from the Pamlico side of our house, across Aunt Martha Oden's yard. It had blown out the window in the upstairs hall at the top of our stairs, and water rose to the third stair step in our house before it began to recede.

Frightened by the advancing tide, recalling the story of Noah's Ark (but not the promise of the rainbow), I buried my face in the ruff of our small, white dog Dobby's neck and cried and prayed that God would save us. When I came downstairs, the tide had lowered on the steps. My prayer had been answered.

Able-bodied men had volunteered or been recruited to raise the piano and our kerosene-run refrigerator with wooden bottle crates from Daddy's store. Other furniture that could be transported up those inside stairs had been moved to the upper floor. But up there, every pot and pan or chamber pot that could be found was situated beneath a leak from the cedar-shingled roof, which did not leak with ordinary showers. Wind whistled under the eves and around the windows, which rattled in their casings. The house swayed in the wind.

We had seen the hurricane light signals the night before. Now the two square red flags with black square centers flapped furiously in the wind.

Following is an account by my mother, Inez Daniels Austin from Hatteras, dated September 17, 1936:

> All day the storm has threatened. Radio reports warned us to move out of the storm area. Lots they know how slim our chances of making a single move to save our lives. The only thing we can do is open our homes to the strangers within our storm-closed gates.

> The people who live nearer the shore may move in nearer the center of the beach land to homes that are no safer per-

haps than those right along the sound or ocean front. One little pitiful mile is the width at the widest point that separates us at this very moment from a very uncertain end.

There is one thing more we can do. We can keep on praying that a Heavenly Father will help us to be sane and sensible at this time and help us to be brave. He calmed the storm on the wind-tossed Galilee. He can do the same today.

Or are we so sinful that we must be shown the power through the elements of a Father's mighty hand?

We hope with every passing moment that the intensity of the storm may lower. We have been given by last report a slim hope that the storm may veer out to sea. Perhaps the land will not get it quite so intensely as we now fear.

May the hand that rules us all wave a gentle wand over the troubled waters and still their tempestuous tossing.

How relieved each heart—how grateful—should the wind quietly lower and no damage come to us and our poor earthly possessions.

The last report says 11:30 is the time set for the most dangerous hour of the storm at this point. We wait with bated breath, hoping against hope that we may not get it so terribly bad here. The tide is over the land, still rising higher and higher.

The Coast Guardsman reports by phone that he is being rocked to sleep in the tower as he watches. They have seen so many storms they seem unafraid. [The phone was in Austin's Store.]

At 12:30 the water is now 14 inches deep in the down stairs rooms. We have the piano 24 inches off the floor, also a davenport on two chairs [wooden]. [Sewing] Machine is on the desk; refrigerator on boxes, Victrola and upholstered chairs on the tables.

The wind is still very strong and flurries seem to indicate that it is increasing in velocity.

Mr. Poe [Rev. John Poe] has gone to bed, also Shanklin. Decatur [cousin] and Josephine look like ostriches on their nest, lying on couch about halfway up to the side of the wall. Mr. [Marion] Holland [Hatteras school teacher] is in another corner on davenport, on a high perch. Andrew sits on a high chair on first stair step, feet propped on second step. I am sitting on a stool, water sloshing up under same.

We had eaten breakfast with our feet in the tide beneath the dining table, had watched the wind drive the tide across the top of the cistern beyond the windows. The demands of the storm had kept us all busy through the day. Later, when the tides had receded, Jo, an older sister, had been among the brave and curious who went to observe the damage and take pictures.

The Northern Methodist Church building and many homes had been washed off their foundations, helped by the wind. Our father's freight boat, Cathleen, had been driven aground and left high and dry near scaffolds where nets were hung to dry. Trees had been uprooted and blown down. Fences were blown over or floated away. Vegetation was destroyed. Caskets and the Hatteras School cistern, which must have been empty, floated out of the ground.

To reduce the likelihood of our house floating, we opened the doors for the tide. As the tide began to recede, every available broom had someone sweeping the silt out with the tide. Water contamination was one of the worst threats to our health. Water in the cisterns, no longer fit to drink, could only be used to clean the remaining mud and grime from the floors. Everything, wet from the tide or the rain, needed time to dry. It took weeks to be rid of the smell of mud and mold.

Following the immediate tasks, others waited to be done. One task was the launching of the Cathleen. Homes had to be hoisted back onto their foundations, and many were raised. Things that had floated away had to be retrieved. Returning to life as usual took awhile. The aftermath of the storm posed special problems for Hatteras residents.

Cisterns had to be cleaned and disinfected with Clorox in anticipation of immediate refreshing rain, or rain that might be days or weeks arriving. Many tasks were beyond my strength and ability and supervision. Some fell to my lot, at least to help. Dressed in our bathing suits, Mona—only six—and I helped clean the smaller of our two cisterns. At first, the tedious, dirty job seemed an adventure. The longer we had to be inside the cistern, the less fun it became. Few homes had indoor plumbing, and outdoor toilets did not require water. However, the refuse from those outdoor toilets became a health hazard when tides rose. Toilets had no pits. Many emptied into the ditches round about. Water in our cisterns became contaminated by salt and who knows what other unsavory critters. Typhoid fever threatened the whole populace of the village.

The American Red Cross brought in drinking water for our immediate needs. They transported it over Oregon Inlet by ferry, down the beach over rutted sand tracks to deliver the five-gallon glass jugs to individual homes from the back of a large truck. Their service continued as long as needed.

In addition, the Red Cross provided typhoid vaccine for our local doctor, H. W. Kenfield, to administer to everyone. We had to have two shots, given at two-week intervals. Standing in line on the lawn outside the door of his small, white office building, adjacent to his lovely home, we waited with dread, all the while swatting mosquitoes.

I had a crush on a boy with brown hair and blue eyes and stood behind him waiting to receive a typhoid shot. When he winced, I imagined his pain and felt happy to share his suffering. Of course, he never knew what a lovesick little girl stood there with him in that line until years later.

Dirty clothes accumulated and needed to be washed. On a small knoll, higher than most ground in the village, near the Atlantic View Hotel, someone drove a pump point for water. Women of the village gathered near the old dipping vat, with galvanized tubs and buckets, soap, bluing, and Red Devil Lye to boil the clothes over an open fire and scrub the boiled clothes on washboards. Near the old dipping vat, which was used when cows and horses that roamed free were rounded up and herded through a solution to kill lice, the women worked in the shade of the yaupon bushes on the sandy hill.

We children played near the empty vat while our mothers worked and chatted. Lines strung between the trees held large pieces like sheets, towels, and men's trousers. When we were allowed to spread small articles on bushes to dry, we felt useful and important. Our reward was a simple lunch of Vienna sausage, crackers, leftover biscuits, and cheese with water.

Few people owned cars or trucks. Transportation of clothes back and forth was not easy for anyone. Had there been means of transporting the water from the dipping vat pump, it could have been taken home for bathing.

Our water supply, vulnerable in all seasons, could be quickly depleted by a running commode or dripping faucet. No wonder I champion water conservation! Dripping faucets and water running away to waste seems a dreadful crime to me.

How elated we were when the first wonderful rain came. We quickly dressed in our swimsuits, grabbed a bar of Ivory soap and headed for the water dripping from the roof of Austin Theater next door to our home. Oh, the luxury of a fresh bath and plentiful water after salt and scarcity! Water means more than money when there is none to buy.

Chapter 3
Daddy Watcher

He didn't talk much. Sometimes at the supper table he'd begin to reminisce, turn his dark eyes to me and ask: "You remember him (her) don't you?" I hated having to say, "No, Daddy I don't remember."

A faded tattoo of a sailing ship on his thin chest spoke of his short stint in the U.S. Navy.

Crippled at nineteen by ankylosing spondylitis—inflammation of the vertebra—which bent his spine into a scythe-like shape, he had visions and ambitions that made him daring, providing for a wife and five offspring.

With twenty-five dollars and a used Daisy barber chair he began his fifty-year business career cutting hair. He quickly progressed to selling general merchandise.

After the store closed at night, he'd sit reading newspapers or books he loved in his chair, his kingdom.

On Sunday evening we'd gather around the radio—"Chase and Sanborn Hour," "Manhattan Merry-Go-Round," "Mr. Anthony." Once we read "Anne of Green Gables" as a family.

An important presence in his benevolent silence, he heard our exchanges but rarely joined our activities as Mama did; but a jigsaw puzzle could pry him from his place and keep him absorbed, with us, for hours.

After congestive heart failure dictated more rest, he slept late while others kept his store, unless he had a building project underway. Then he would arise early, eager to be on site to supervise. Other times, many came with questions that he, propped high on pillows, answered from his bed.

He knew the ways of wood and engines. Once he dreamed how to repair a pesky motor, awoke, and fixed it. He built three boats: "Ramona," "Sybil" and another dubbed "Blue Mud" for its bright, azure interior, that Mama had wanted to name "Jomarsha" for Josephine, Marjorie, and Shanklin, the other children

He oversaw building Gooseville Gun Club; Hatteras Girls Club, first acquiring a dredge to build its site; Massoletti's Cottage; Austin Theater; Durant Motor Court; and actively participated in some phases of remodeling and expansion of Austin's General Merchandise Store and our living quarters into five apartments.

He was secretary-treasurer for the inactive Woodmen of the World Lodge; they'd come to his store office to pay insurance year after year, or to have him write to claim a member's death benefit.

He owned the nets and boat, "Blue Mud," that brother Monroe and another fished. Sitting by the chimney in the store, he sometimes tied nets.

He owned a freight boat, Cathleen, that carried fish to Elizabeth City, North Carolina, and transported freight back to Hatteras village. His youngest brother, Horton, was once its captain.

Once his brother Nacie's daughter, Ruby, and I took that boat trip with a giant sea turtle we tended with water all the way from Hatteras to Elizabeth City, where Daddy and Uncle Nacie received us when we arrived aboard the Cathleen. Our charge became someone's turtle soup.

He tended Sunday dinner while we went to church. I worried about his soul and gave him a copy of St. John's Gospel that Mrs. Charlotte

Ballance gave me for memorizing "The Beatitudes" in Sunday School. But once, when he and I were returning from a trip, he drove to Oregon Inlet and we slept all night in the car to catch Sunday morning's first ferry so that I'd not lose my church school attendance pin. Years later, he told me of his conversion experience and his disillusionment with one of God's vessels.

"Pappy" to his grandchildren and Daddy to his own, I never doubted the love he never spoke. Hadn't he painted a white doll black because his four year old kept requesting he bring her a black baby from Elizabeth City?

I remember his tolerance and loyalty over all the years, his reliable strength and availability to his eight siblings, to his family and his friends.

Thirteen of us filled the house that 1948 summer. He piled bowls high with ice cream from the store each night as we gathered in the living room, eating all his ice cream profit and more!

We knew what he expected of us: to be honest, respectable, respectful, hardworking, helpful, and kind to others.

Watching the fluid flow into his veins at Albemarle Hospital, Elizabeth City, I prayed it would become the communion body and blood of Christ. I believe a merciful God came with others to take him HOME Sunday, October 7, 1962.

"Sometimes he seems so close to me, I feel I can speak to him," sister Jo said on his birth date one February 20th, as we shared our gratitude for our 135 pound patriarch, who looms large in our lives and memories.

Andrew Shanklin Austin
February 20, 1889–October 7, 1962.

This piece has appeared previously in *Echoes,* a publication of the Chapel Hill Senior Center's Writers' Discussion Group.

Chapter 4
Hatteras Merchant

❧

A merchant for over fifty years, my father learned a lot about reality and human nature. A poem he had framed in a handmade frame, prominently displayed by the store office door, spoke of an idealism in which men would meet and trust one another:

If I knew you and you knew me,
'Tis seldom we would disagree...

Stores were gathering places back in the twenties and thirties. Daddy's store stayed open to catch last minute trade and late opinions. Such good conversation went on around the stove in the wintertime. In the summer, the same location drew the usual crowd to sit on two handcrafted benches and exchange views or get into some heated discussion.

Sometimes when things were slow or someone else waited on the trade, Daddy could be found by the oak roll-top desk catching up on things in the office of the store. One Saturday evening a man of the community came in his office to ask about opening an account. Most folks let accounts run from month to month and came in once a month to "settle up." Daddy knew this man too well and asked him, "Haven't you been trading with Dolph Burrus?"

"Yes, sir, I have."

Not to beat around the bush, nor waste his time nor the man's, he came right to the point. "Has Dolph turned you away because you haven't been paying your bills?"

Probably embarrassed, the man must have been more surprised when Daddy continued, "If I take you on and you don't pay me, I'll have to turn you away. I think the best thing for me to do for both of us is to give you this."

Daddy shifted on one hip in the oak swivel desk chair, reached into the pocket of his pants, and handed the man a ten dollar bill, at a time when ten dollars would buy an ample supply of groceries for a family for a week.

Did the man thank him? Perhaps. Perhaps not!

Telling Mama about it later, Daddy laughed, pleased to have found a bargain of a different sort. Laughter for Daddy came rarely. When it did, his eyes crinkled with amusement, and his breaths came in catching gasps in his throat. He could hardly finish his story.

"Do you know what he did?" He laughed again until tears came to his eyes. "He took the ten dollars I'd given him and walked out of my store to spend it somewhere else."

No, Daddy was not implying the man would spend it on other than groceries. It was the joke on him that caused him such amusement.

Finally sober, he pondered the matter, chuckled a little and said, "It was a bargain for all that!"

This piece has appeared previously in *State* magazine.

Chapter 5
A Proud Heritage
❧

As I begin to relate my early memories, I marvel at how good life has been, in spite of hearing loss after a bout of measles in the seventh grade and other obstacles that could have made my life less than successful. Yet, I graduated from high school and college, married a handsome, desirable man, mothered his three sons, and shared his life and success. During his life and after his death, one of the hardest events of my whole life after thirty-three years of marriage, I worked as a hospital pharmacist. When I retired in 1990, I had worked for Durham County Hospital Corporation for twenty-three years.

As I have written, I have become aware of my good fortune in the parents I had and the place I lived. Even more important is my knowing I have a loving Heavenly Father, whom I learned to follow early. His hand has been on my life from birth.

The fourth child, born into a family of five children and a mobile, changing household, I have done what I saw my parents do. They made the best of every situation, good or bad. Responsible and loving parents, they were too busy to pamper us, but were alert to our needs. However, for the day-to-day things we had to learn self-sufficiency and to solve our own problems.

Sometime along the way, I realized that in our early, busy household we were surrounded most of the time by others and were seldom alone as a family. Our father's general merchandise business was as much a part of our everyday life as breakfast, dinner, and supper. We were in and out of the store like another room of the house, which essentially it was. Seeing people from the village come and go, we became oriented into the business. We learned that the customer is always right, at least always worthy of our respect and consideration. With tasks appropriate to our ages, each did his or her share in the house to keep things moving along; and when older, each did an apprenticeship in the store at one time or another. Important in different ways to many within the home and community, I felt needed and appreciated, even without words of praise. When I became a college student, with only my own affairs to consider, life seemed strange.

Affluence or fame never impressed me greatly, not then and not now. People of influence became part of our lives while we sat on our small island, with the Atlantic to the east and the Pamlico Sound on the west. I felt fortunate to have a mother who had taught school and a father who knew how to do so many things and owned businesses. We had advantages many in the Hatteras community, a fishing village of five hundred souls, did not have. After we were grown, a cousin commented reflectively, "Your family had more than most people of the community, but you had to work harder than we did."

True, we did! We had our responsibilities. We received what we needed by helping the total operation run smoothly. Interesting people who surrounded us messed up many dishes and had to be fed. Their rooms had to be kept clean and their beds changed regularly. We were expected to help.

Our mothers belonged to Lend a Hand Clubs and Dare County Extension Clubs. We little girls mimicked them, formed our own clubs, and learned from them to sew, crochet, knit, and cook. Our 4-H

Clubs, administered by the state and county, encouraged us to be thrifty homemakers; and boys raised on farms learned about raising pigs and cows and other livestock, no doubt. How Hatteras Island boys won points I don't know. Maybe they grew gardens. Girls prepared meals, sewed, and did other home tasks for their credits. My brother's reaction to one of my efforts, stuffed onions, was disappointing. "Sybil, they would be okay if you had something else to go with them!"

My mother's description of her home life in Wanchese, North Carolina, made me want what our household seemed to lack. Probably, however, in the day by day of the late 1800s, her fisherman-farmer-family knew more difficulties than mine did in the 1930s. We still had rain barrels, artesian wells, and cisterns. The laundry, an arduous task, began by boiling clothes in a galvanized washtub over an open fire out of doors. We did not have a cauldron. Next the clothes, once removed from the boiling water, were scrubbed on washboards with homemade lye soap, rinsed thoroughly, and hung to dry. Monday washday, if it did not rain or storm, took all day long. But we did not have to knit socks or spin cloth as her mother had done. When Mama acquired an electric washing machine with a ringer on the top, the task still took all day.

Our outdoor toilets attracted the concern of health authorities. Under one of the New Deal programs of President Franklin Delano Roosevelt, our backyard bloomed with new, pine privies, which were to be distributed to the many people needing them. These were built under the supervision of Mr. Corey, from another part of North Carolina. Even our family had one erected over a deep, closed pit for the first time. With toilets no longer over open ground or dumping into ditches or creeks, our community enjoyed improved sanitation and less exposure to threats from raw sewage.

Ice, shipped from a distance, was not always available, even if the home had an icebox. A hunk of ice might be wrapped in burlap and stored in a galvanized washtub or some other container. To obtain a piece of ice meant a trip to the fish house. We had no iceman. Refrigeration awaited Rural Electrification, which came later in our lives.

Kerosene lamps, the mantle lamps giving the best light, were usual. Our home had electric lights, a bulb in the middle of the ceiling of each room, because Daddy had a Delco in the engine house that was started when the sun went down at night. I do not know how late in the life of the house the electricity came. However, much left over from another century remained part of our lives.

What caught my imagination about my mother's childhood had to do with the gathering of the family in the evening after supper. Her father, George Charles Daniels, would make shoe repairs and sing songs of the five hundred he claimed to know, while her mother, Margaret Johnson, would spin, knit, or darn. My sense of poverty did not involve the tangible. Our main time together as a family was at mealtimes, for which I am grateful. Oral history was shared then. And we were joined in purpose by the work we shared. Many modern families miss these opportunities. My need, or desire, for family closeness and my idealization of my grandfather's family were frustrated by the fact that Daddy did not sing.

Word-of-mouth news traveled fast in our community, even without telephones, and kept us aware of the events in the surrounding area. When Daddy heard that one of the surfmen from Creeds Hill Lifesaving Station had found and brought in turtle eggs, he took us to see them. Today children go to museums of the sea to see turtle eggs. Sea turtles are an endangered species, and their eggs are protected.

Shipwrecks along the North Carolina Coast waters abreast of Hatteras Island have caused Diamond Shoals to be called the Graveyard of the Atlantic. David Stick, in his book "Graveyard of the Atlantic," documented a considerable number of shipwrecks off the North Carolina Coast from 1526 to 1945. When Daddy heard the news of one exposed, he took the family up to Gull Shoal to see the four-masted schooner, G. A. Kohler, which came ashore August 23,

1933, during a hurricane.

Modern communication, improvements in navigation, as well as better weather surveillance, make it far less likely now that a vessel will be caught and run aground in that dangerous area. Every navigator knows to avoid the rough waters off Cape Hatteras in the area of Diamond Shoals, if possible.

Our parents taught us to be honest, responsible, kind, worthwhile human beings. Hard workers themselves, they taught us not to shirk hard work. They sacrificed to raise five children and to send us from the small fishing village for advanced education.

Brother Shanklin (A.S. Austin, Jr.) never wanted more than to finish high school at Oak Ridge Military Academy. Marjorie Hope finished her last two high school years at Peace College in Raleigh, North Carolina. She had a one-year commercial course at Woman's College of the University of North Carolina at Greensboro and an additional commercial course in Raleigh "to build her confidence." After that, she took a secretarial job in High Point, North Carolina, at Tomlinson Furniture Manufacturing Company, where she met her husband, Clifford Curtis Newton, Jr.

Josephine had two years at Woman's College before transferring to Carolina to graduate with a degree in journalism. She worked as a journalist for The Daily Advance in Elizabeth City, North Carolina, a short time before marrying her childhood sweetheart, Carlos Desmond Oden of Hatteras, who was then serving in the United States Navy during World War II.

When my turn came to attend college, after a year between high school and college, I also attended Woman's College. As a sophomore, I transferred to the University of North Carolina at Chapel Hill. There I met Donald Edmund Skakle of Waltham, Massachusetts, in the fall of 1945. We were married February 7, 1947. I graduated in 1949 with a B. S. degree in Pharmacy.

Ramona (Mona) went all four years at Woman's College, graduated with a degree in Home Economics in June 1950, and married Virgil

Archibald Wilson of Rural Hall, North Carolina, the following week. She took her first job with the Dairy Council of Durham, North Carolina, and proceeded to help put him through the first graduating class of The University of North Carolina Medical School.

Our mother had attended Woman's College in 1910-11, when it had been known as North Carolina Normal School. Elizabeth Newton, Marjorie's only child, furthered the tradition her grandmother began and that her four daughters had continued.

With a Dare County certificate, obtained by passing a county administered test, and without a college degree, our mother taught school in three counties. In response to an inquiry of J. P. Hollis regarding her state retirement benefits, October 9, 1958, she wrote, "I have had twenty years of teaching service, three years before marriage, 1910-1914, in Perquimans County, Beaufort County, and Dare County. In 1922 I was again teaching in Dare County. I taught three years at this time. I took time off to raise and graduate five children.

"In 1945 I began again teaching and attending school. Teaching was continuous except the 1952-1953 session when I attended the spring quarter and summer school and helped a daughter (Mona) take care of her first son.

"The next year I was back again and resigned August 26, 1958, because of my husband's health."

She asked to withdraw her benefits even while she expressed a desire to teach again at some future time. She fought to see her children have the education she wanted so badly for herself and saw they received all they would accept.

Having been out of teaching many years, she began teaching again during the shortage of teachers during World War II years to help pay for Mona's and my college costs. She attended summer schools and took correspondence courses to upgrade her Dare County Teacher's Certificate. After retiring in 1958, she was called back after a terrible storm known as the Ash Wednesday Storm, 1963, which cut the northern end of Hatteras Island off from the consolidated school in

Buxton. Daddy had died in October of 1962, at seventy-two. She taught in Avon for several months, staying at the Avon Hotel, until the inlet was filled in, roads redone, and the children from the northern end of the island could be transported again to Cape Hatteras School at Buxton.

Three years later, Mama, approaching her seventy-fifth birthday, returned to Carolina in an attempt to get her coveted college degree. Modern civilization, conflict in the family, and ill health, aggravated by deep grief over our father's death, defeated her. She had won one language requirement in Spanish before she gave up her ambitious venture.

Despite my marriage as a junior, an unplanned pregnancy and birth of our first son eighteen months later, I did graduate. I had taken fewer courses than I needed due to my pregnancy. After Eddie's birth in July, I had to wait until the following spring semester to complete my college requirements. While I waited, I took American Literature by correspondence for an elective credit.

I studied hard and thought deeply. I learned much by reading early authors, beginning with Bradford, Cooper, and Conrad. Struggling to answer questions by correspondence, I learned much about human nature and emotion, especially from Joseph Conrad's "Heart of Darkness" and James Fenimore Cooper's "The Deer Slayer." I gained great appreciation for the literature of my country, and for my own life and background, which included a Native American great-grandmother. I graduated in 1949 not cum laude but cum infant.

My parents, my role models, deserve my praise. Their lives exemplified courage and determination, which I needed to reach my goal. My parents' lives rather than their counsel acted as an impetus for me. Their victories over personal adversity and deprivation had become part of who they were and who I am. How could I quit short of my degree goal with such parentage?

Hatteras on the Outer Banks of North Carolina, a great training ground, had prepared me to persevere and to succeed in life beyond my limitations and hardships. Bridges have enabled the changes that have made Hatteras a prosperous, attractive place for others to live and work. My life was forged there before bridges.

Hatteras is favored as a place for vacationing tourists from all over the United States and beyond. The moving of the Cape Hatteras Lighthouse the summer of 1999 focused the attention of the world on the place I will always call "home." I am grateful for my proud heritage of parents and place, and so I have written in these pages about my family and growing up at Hatteras.

Chapter 6
Starting on a Shoestring

❧

*D*addy once said that he would have liked to have studied to be a doctor, if his background had given him a choice. His father William Wheeler Austin, born April 23, 1860, supported a wife, seven sons, and two daughters on his small U. S. Lifesaving Service pay. When my father was of school age, one man had responsibility in the small rural community of Hatteras for teaching reading, writing, and arithmetic to a mixed group of children. The education my father received may have been equivalent to a fourth grade education today. So Daddy did not have an opportunity to study medicine. However, he did well with the choices he made.

Andrew Shanklin Austin had to have been very young when he joined the United States Navy. An impressive tattoo of a sailing vessel on his thin chest recalled that time. By nineteen he had received an honorable discharge from the service. My understanding is that he had to leave the service due to a back condition, which caused severe pain and drawing. His sister Beatrice once told me how his family propped his body on pillows between two chairs to help relieve his excruciating agony during that time.

His birth family, and later, Mama and others speculated about probable causes. Some supposed his staying wet on the trip back from

South America on a naval ship might have caused it. Others voiced the opinion that he may have injured his back while employed at the porpoise factory, located in three different locations on Hatteras Island, near or at Hatteras, between 1700s and until 1929, except for occasional interruptions. While not active in 1902, it must have been during that time between 1907 through 1914 when William F. Nye Company of New Bedford, Massachusetts, operated the fishery. Daddy and his father both worked there sometime during those years.

Lou Angell's article "The Porpoise Factory" (*The State*, October, 1981), reported: "The last operator was a Hatteras Village native, William Harris (Harrison) Rolinson, who died in 1928. His widow, Mrs.Theresa Rolinson, carried on the effort for awhile after his death, but finally gave it up and sold the equipment (nets, boats, etc.) that her husband had owned."

Daddy, just a youth, would lie on his stomach on the factory dock, reach down, grab a porpoise tail from the hands of the fisherman and flip it over his shoulder onto the dock. It was weight lifting with a porpoise purpose! Porpoise products included heavy blubber oil and hides to be tanned for leather goods. The most valuable and smallest harvest of oil, called jawbone, watch, or melon oil, was used to lubricate the workings of watches and clocks.

Years later, we learned that his condition, a rare one, had been caused by neither of these experiences of his. He and at least two other men on Hatteras Island were similarly afflicted by ankylosing spondylitis, or Marie-Stümpell Disease. In the disease, the small joints of the spine diminish and fuse, shortening the spine, causing the spine to curve, and resulting in constriction of the chest cavity. The curvature of Daddy's back looked to be about sixty degrees.

An early picture of Daddy shows him among others in a hospital ward or treatment room at Hot Springs, Arkansas. Mama used to say she married him expecting to live in Arkansas. On their eleven-day trip in July of 1936 across country, they visited Hot Springs and spent two hours at Buckstaff Bathhouse, where the picture was taken.

They, four of Mama's relatives and Mama and Daddy, were in a four door sedan, before air conditioning, enroute to visit Mama's brother Caswell and his family in Oakland, California, and had stopped off for Daddy to revisit and for Mama to see where he had been treated, which may have been before they ever met. Maybe not.

Apparently, the U. S. government sent Daddy there for treatment. The picture shows a handsome man with dark hair, piercing dark eyes, and high cheekbones. It is supposed he inherited these features from his grandmother, Sally Anne Fulcher, a full-blooded American Indian, probably Hatterask Indian tribe, or possibly Algonquin.[9]

When Mama first met Daddy, she and Sally Montague, the daughter of her half sister Lucetta, had been guests of his sisters Beatrice and Lovie. Sally had told Inez (Mama) that Andrew Austin was a very handsome man. But when Mama first saw his crippled condition she did not agree with Sally.

After his discharge from the Navy, Daddy sometimes fished up and down the coastal waters of Hatteras and nearby community of Wanchese, where my mother lived with her large family. After their meeting, while fishing from Wanchese, he visited Inez Lynn and enjoyed the company of her father George Charles Daniels so much that she once asked him, "Who did you come to see, Dad or me?"

She complained to her father: "You two have so much to talk about that I never get chance to talk to him."

Later, when she and Daddy married, her father George, obviously fond of Andrew and disturbed by their unhappy arguments, advised, "Daughter, I've observed that the hogs that squeal the least are the ones that get the most swill!"

Besides fishing, Daddy had another interest, a new business. He purchased a building from his Uncle Dock and without truck, tractor, or bulldozer, moved the shop from his uncle's yard to a lot some distance away. That took inventive planning, more ingenious than when Mama and I moved the chicken house to another area in the back yard. Just how we did that and how they moved that shop, I do not know. The old adage says, "Where there is a will, there is a way!"

Maybe the old horse Deck helped move the building, guiding it through that soft sand to a lot close to the road and across from Gaskins Cemetery, in front of a house Almy Burrus built for his bride Lovie O'Neal and himself, property owned by Mark Oden since 1989. Before the pavement came to the village, sometime after 1958, the sand ruts were deepest and softest in front of Gaskins Cemetery, located today on the sandy knoll next to Midgett's Garage.

One night when I was a child, alone and very scared, I had had my progress hampered by that sand. Mama said, "I'm not afraid of the dead. I'm afraid of the wagging tongues of the living." Her philosophy did not help me that evening. I was scared and could not get by the dead in that graveyard fast enough.

With a building, twenty-five dollars, and a red velvet-covered barber chair, bought second-hand in Washington, North Carolina, Daddy began his first business in 1908. The chair had a metal plate on the front, which identified it as a Daisy. Eugene Beinghaus, the manufacturer, built barber furniture between 1904-1912 in Cincinnati, Ohio.

The old barber chair, now owned by Donald Edmund Skakle, Jr., is a treasured family heirloom. Head and footrests were lost or discarded a long time ago, unfortunately. The chair itself has worn several different covers. A black, grained oilcloth replaced the original red velvet cover. Mama and Daddy together re-covered it in the deep blue denim it still wears. The chair is a reminder of other years, other ways, and other people, who found it a favorite place to be—to read the Grit, a weekly newspaper still in existence; to wait for trade; to listen to the customers; or to watch people go by on the road in front of Austin's Store.

As soon as he could, Daddy diversified and expanded his business. Besides cutting hair, he did a lively trade on Saturday, when the "fellers" got slicked up to go courting the local girls and needed socks, bow ties, disposable shirt collars and cuffs, shoe strings, and candy.

Mrs. Lovie Burrus, past ninety when she died, remembered when she was pregnant with her first child, Lucille, and had craved peanut butter kisses bought at "Ander's Shop."

He sold ices and milk shakes. The basic ingredient for both delicacies was ice that came from Elizabeth City by freight boat to ice fish, which were in turn shipped back to the city to be shipped to northern markets. Returning from Elizabeth City, the freight boat Cathleen would be loaded with freight and more ice, to ice more fish and furnish ice for village needs.

With a hand-held ice shaver, he shaved ice until it filled the metal container. This he dumped into a glass and poured sweet flavored syrup over it to make the ices. Some of that syrup survived until I was a girl. That orange syrup had a flavor like none since savored. Besides orange, he had root beer, strawberry, vanilla, and chocolate.

Daddy's milk shakes were without ice cream. Made with ice, canned milk and flavored syrup, with everything dumped into a quart Mason jar, or some other appropriate sized container, and shaken until the whole became cold, frothy, and delicious.

In my father's generation, ice cream was synonymous with Tom Angell, the only black citizen of the village. The Angells, a white family, found Tom when he was eight years old in Washington, North Carolina. With his mother's approval, they brought him to Hatteras, where he served the family all their lives and, eventually, inherited their Hatteras property.

There had been a few blacks on the Island in earlier years. Early census and estate records show that at least one family owned a few slaves. Once while Daddy and I were sharing the dishwashing chore, he told me that the few black families who lived in the village earlier had moved away a long time before. So Tom had no friends of his own race until Mr. Dolph Burrus hired Lou to come and help his wife, Lucy, take care of their family. Their daughter, Marian, and I were little girls together when Lou, possibly Louise, and Tom kept one another company.

When my father and his friends were young, they enjoyed gathering with someone special to eat ice cream at Tom's, who was a bit older but still young, on a Sunday afternoon in the summer. Tom entertained them by playing his violin or organ. Once, as a little girl, I remember eating ice cream and cake at Tom's one Sunday afternoon. But by then, Tom did not make ice cream regularly. There were ice cream people in my life. I'll tell you about them further along in my story.

Even though he had not studied economics, Daddy understood the principle of supply and demand. He reinvested his profits, kept his capital working, and strictly disciplined himself to use only his profits to expand. Loans were out of the question for him and other Islanders. He believed prompt payment of debt a moral obligation and a privilege. "Money owed, even if it's in my hand, does not belong to me!" he said.

By 1918, four years after his marriage, December 9, 1914, to Inez Lynn Daniels, he had erected a two-storied building on property, "one acre more or less," purchased from his uncle, Dock Oden, who lived next door. He named the store A. S. Austin, General Merchandise and Dry Goods Store. With more space, Daddy diversified further and became more and more an entrepreneur.

Before the living quarters and store were built, two other married siblings, their spouses, their children, and four younger brothers lived with parents Wheeler and Mogieannah, as well as Inez, Andrew, and their toddler son Shank. Conflicts and overcrowding wearied everyone.

In 1918, a worldwide flu epidemic caused many deaths. That year, before the birth of their second child, Marjorie Hope, on March 28th, Mama and Daddy moved to their unfinished home. Mama had become conscious that not being born at Hatteras, she had an "outsider" status, even though Wanchese was in the same county and about 60 miles away. She was very happy to have her own space, however inferior it might be for a while.

In the new dwelling, a door from the living room opened into the store. There were advantages and disadvantages of living and breathing the business as they did. It enabled Daddy to oversee the household and the store, giving Mama emotional security and support when needed. It gave Daddy her energy and physical help when he had to be out of the store.

Mama used to tell the story about the day she kept store, with two little children to watch, for him to join other men who were going aboard a shipwreck to salvage what they could. All day she ironed, waited on the trade, and took care of the children, expecting Daddy to bring home flat wear or some other wonderful treasure. When he returned, with pockets full of matches, he explained that he kept hoping to find something better. After she got over being angry and frustrated, Mama's sense of humor let her see the irony of it. It made a good story, and our Mama was a fine storyteller.

Some articles, like the bathtub, in our home came from wrecked ships. They became cherished possessions. Family members now own two ship washstands, which were used in bedrooms for many years. Four lovely oak, ship drawers—two long ones and two short ones—were built into a frame under a long counter in the upstairs hall to hold linens. Below the drawers were cabinets. Part of the same structure, on the end toward the long hall that gave access to the bedrooms and upstairs living room, a bookcase with glass doors held Mama's precious books.

When Daddy rebuilt the house between 1945-1950, he used all he could from the original building. All the old tongue and grove from the old house backed the plaster board on the walls and ceilings of the renovated house, and the drawers and bookcase were given a prominent place, grouped together in a compact stationary piece in what is now the fourth apartment of Austin's 1908 Guesthouse. Few buildings are sturdier than that one built of old and new.

Above the store area were five bedrooms and a guest living room. The main living quarters, in the wing to the right and at right angle to the store section, had a roof lower than the one covering the other space. Beneath the lower roof downstairs were living room, kitchen, and Mama's sewing-room. An inside stairway from the downstairs living room gave access to the hall area over the store and the five bedrooms and living room. To the left and past the oak ship drawers were two or three steps leading down to the two bedrooms over the living room and kitchen. Later this fashionable arrangement became known as "split level."

Mona and I had the bedroom over the kitchen, reached by going through the one where Mama and Daddy slept. We slept there many years, until we became "of age" to claim the bedrooms on the hall—each different—where we had been born. However, we slept around quite a bit, too. When Mona and I broke the iron bedstead springs by diving together from the head of the bed, we were sleeping together in a room down the hall that neither of us claimed. Another time when Jo had pneumonia, she slept in our room next to our parents' room to be near Mama's care. And the night Mona was born, November 12, 1930, I slept with Aunt Rado in the front bedroom off the upstairs living room. It was so cold that we slept in our clothes, a delight to a four-year-old child. So, circumstances caused us to shift about the house. We had many choices. However, we each had a room. Mama told us Daddy eagerly waited outside the room where we were born, ready to receive and hold each new arrival.

At some point, a sixth small bedroom on the hall at the top of the inside stairway had been claimed for a bathroom for the whole house. To supplement the bathroom there were chamber pots and wash bowls with pitchers and those ship washstands in the five bedrooms on the hall. One July in the fifties, when the July 4th tourist trade filled every room in the house, the chamber pots and bowls and pitchers were needed, as they had been many other times.

Before Daddy acquired an electric pump, water had to be pumped up by hand to a wooden tank in the attic. By gravity it supplied the bathroom on the level below. He hired husky young fellows to pump the water. Jarvis Midgette, son of a cousin, Sally Oden, pumped water for him. Jarvis, in December, 1998, told me about it. He and others sent up to pump got into Daddy's home brew. That was the end of their employment.

Mama was responsible for stopping Daddy's production of home brew. She put kerosene in his mash. He confronted her with, " Inez, you've done it now!"

"Yes, and I'll do it again. I'm not going to raise my kids around that stuff."

Therefore, a wonderful, tan stone crock served to collect trash in the store for years after. But the production of home brew ended then and there.

Mona and I loved the attics. There were two. One over our bedroom area had no windows. Listening to the rain on the roof and drinking purloined, canned orange juice on top of a big wooden drawer holding Mama's colorful quilts is a vivid memory. Another is of the odor of the stalks of bananas hanging in the upper attic, which had windows at either end. After a banana ship broke up off the coast, bunches and bunches of bananas washed ashore. Every home had bananas for a while.

My favorite place in the house was the upstairs living room. With my knees hanging over the arm of a large mohair chair, even during a hurricane when the house swayed in the wind, I could hide away there and read. Some little red books (The World's One Hundred Best Short Stories, in ten volumes, copyright 1927) stored in a desk in the upstairs living room, provided very interesting reading when I had no other book. I read them not knowing that I was reading some of the best literature available.

Even before we began to date, we sometimes played games on the floor, like bob jacks and cards, in the upstairs living room with our friends in warm weather. In later years, we were permitted to have our friends and dates visit there, even to heat the room by the oil heater. No longer needed for boarders, that room served as the equivalent of the extra parlor, used for company, found in many homes on the island.

From that room, a door with a glass panel at top, which Mona ran a broom handle through chasing me, led to two descending steps to a wonderful porch. Enclosed by a partially open wooden railing, the porch overlooked the center of Hatteras Village and provided a great place from which to watch the world beyond.

Next door to the left stood the Methodist parsonage. The Slash Bridge, just beyond, and other dwellings stood between our eyes and the mighty Atlantic. We heard the sound of the surf. To the right and a shorter distance away, we had a view of Pamlico Sound. Across the road stood the Hatteras School. Situated to the left of the school were Hatteras Methodist Church, Hatteras Girls Club, and The Slash. To the right of the school stood Loran Ballance's "filling station" and pool hall. Across the road to the right stood Burrus' Store, now Burrus Red and White. Around the corner and across the Oden's yard, the Hatteras Weather Station, an important structure, stood next to Damon Gray's home and barbershop. We were in the center of our world.

As children, Mona and I played on that porch often. We found a wonderful knothole that was just right to spit through, to target unsuspecting persons coming out of Daddy's store. It only took one direct hit to spoil our fun.

A wonderful stairway from the upstairs porch descended along the east, outside wall of the store for our guests and for us. During clean-up days and spring-cleaning, the upper porch provided railings to air rugs and bedding, and the porch itself provided room for mattresses and feather beds to have the sun and fresh air. Spring housecleaning, which I hated, was an exhausting event that lasted for days and days. Soap, water, and paint freshened our surroundings.

To the left of the front door downstairs, an alcove held a sink, hand pump, and a towel on a roller. We secured water from the cistern on the eastern side of the house. When water was low, we had to prime the pump before any water could be drawn. When the water level fell very low, we sometimes drew up "wigglers," destined to become adult mosquitoes. That event signaled the need to clean the cistern thoroughly before the next rain.

Few people owned cars or other means of transportation until after World War II. Daddy's customers would bring or send their grocery orders to the store to be filled and delivered. Filled, put in boxes, these orders were delivered, first by Old Deck and the cart, later by vehicles of various description that Daddy owned over the years. My first driving lesson, given by cousin Wheeler Ballance, was on an old flat-bodied truck with four gears. The day I lost a muffler, I was driving a four-door Ford sedan. When George and Travis Austin brought it back to us, they became heroes. When my husband, sons, and I lived and worked there between 1954-1958, a brown jeep, probably World War II surplus, filled the need.

Austin's General Merchandise and Dry Goods Store had a varied inventory. There were little brass fittings for engines; gaskets and fan belts for those newfangled cars; nails, screws, dry goods and notions; patent medicines, cosmetics, paint, some clothing, school supplies, a few pots and pans, even soles for shoes; also, gum boots—with and without the bibs that covered the whole body. These were called waders and were used by hunters when they went out in the blinds to shoot geese. He sold nets and rope by the pound. People sent their five-gallon cans for kerosene, for most homes used kerosene stoves for cooking. A raw potato made an excellent stopper if their oil container did not have a cap.

While sales came mainly from the food line, fresh meat was a rare commodity and came later in the history of the village when a man nicknamed "Pork Chops" brought it onto the island from up in Currituck County. Cured meat—slab bacon, sausage, ham, and salt pork—had been available because these could be handled without refrigeration. Mama told us how welcome the fresh pork from her father, sent after a pig killing, had been to Daddy's family when they lived there.

Many had their own chickens, and fish were plentiful. Scallops were sometimes available—clams, oysters, and shrimp too. However, as a little girl, I do not remember shrimp, and I cannot tell you why. Maybe there were no shrimp nets in Hatteras then. But steamed oysters were delicious and messy.

Molasses and vinegar were delivered to the store in fifty gallon wooden barrels. Early I learned the meaning of "slower than molasses in January," when I had to grind out a quart in cold weather. In hot weather it might ferment and boil over the side, putting Daddy's overhead onto the floor.

Cheese came in hoops. With experience I learned to cut a pound pretty close. On the big old scale with weights to be added to a hook on its side, it would be placed on a thick glass platform to be balanced against the weights.

Chicken feed came in fifty-pound bags. Sometimes the feed came in cloth that could be used for making clothing or bedding. The feed was sold by the peck or quart. Burlap bags held most of the feed delivered to the stores. These we children used sometimes when we decided to build a tent.

In the springtime, there were garden seeds and fertilizer. Some used seaweed as good mulch for the sandy soil that did not hold moisture well. Daddy planted a big crop of sweet potatoes one year. Mama always had a few collards planted somewhere. However, gardens were not the rule for our family. There were too many other tasks.

Little by little, Daddy progressed. Besides his store, he owned a freight boat, captained for many years by Victor Ballance with Nye Rollinson as mate. Later, after his youngest brother, Horton, came home from the Coast Guard, he acted as captain for a number of years.

Daddy also owned nets and a fishing boat he had built by himself in the back yard. These were utilized by his oldest brother, Monroe, and Edward Austin. Boat and nets, maintained by Daddy, accounted for his third of the operation.

Daddy had an accurate, if not usual, bookkeeping method. Bookkeeping required time. Besides the business end of the store, he had many other interests that made him restless and required time for him to pursue them. Therefore, he needed others to do the work of the store. Many different persons worked as manager or clerk over the fifty years his store remained in operation.

His brother Nacie worked with him for a while during the early Depression years. However, Nacie longed to become a master carpenter. That was his love and became his livelihood.

Herman Burrus, the oldest child of Daddy's cousin Blanch, who married Luther Burrus, managed the business for a time after having tired of teaching school. But when the Hatteras Development Company, an ice and electric plant, came into being, Herman went to work for Tom Eaton and later moved to Norfolk with his family to become a successful accountant there.

Brother Shank, before he was conscripted during World War II, managed and clerked in the store, as well as taking care of Austin Theater, his business. I clerked in the store and managed Austin Theater my last year in high school and the year between high school and college when Shank went into the Army to serve in India. During summer vacations, I had worked in the store before.

My husband Don served in the capacity of manager-clerk from 1954-58. Many others of the family did apprenticeships in store business: all of the sisters, Margie's daughter Beth Newton, and Shank's wife Ruby Meekins. Scores of others—Wheeler Ballance, Minerva Stowe Fagley, Clyde Austin, Mae Styron, Brittie Burrus, Vera Robinson, Minnie Gillikin Ballance, and others—were employed for short or long stays.

The store office was Daddy's domain. But he loved being in the center of good conversation when the men gathered around the stove during cold weather. Or, in the summer when the stove had been stored, they gathered where the stove had been to sit on Daddy's improvised benches, still in existence. They exchanged moral views regarding politics and government, reviewed community activities and the effects of the weather on fishing and fish prices.

Daddy did not shy away from a good argument. I doubt he chose an argument arbitrarily. However, having taken a position, he did not desert it easily. He would listen to a contrary viewpoint and consider it. Only when he had became convinced of his error, could he abandon his first position. If not, his integrity required him to stand firm. Before I understood, I thought that trait of his was stubbornness. Daddy might have made a good lawyer, if not a doctor. He was a man his children and grandchildren admired and respected. He lived his life bravely and well.

Everyone depended on fishing for a livelihood. Daddy's brother Fred, two years younger, acted as a fish broker. He bought fish. He would often come in to call markets in Elizabeth City for prices to know what he could afford to pay. There were few phones, none in homes, and those that were available were on the single party line. Three rings signaled a call to Austin Store. (An exception may have been the Hatteras Weather Bureau line.)

All the siblings of my father did well. All were honest, hardworking individuals. Family ties are deep and passionate, evidenced by Austin Family biennial reunion of the Austin Family descendants, who continue to carry forward the traits of industry and ingenuity fostered by Hatteras Island ancestors.[10]

Chapter 7

The Daniels Side of the Family

༄

W illiam Daniels, Sr., arrived on Roanoke Island around
1765. A sea captain, he was granted a piece of land known
as Bodie Island on the beach abreast of Roanoke Island for
running slaves from across the ocean. This same William Daniels,
Sr., served as a captain during an Indian uprising in 1771. In 1784
Daniels obtained a grant of 738 acres of land on Roanoke Island's
east side from Governor Alexander Martin and built the first house
on the south end of Roanoke Island.

Records from Currituck County—Dare County was not formed
until 1870—show that land on Roanoke Island, part of a royal grant
to Sir William Berkeley, was deeded to his son William Daniels, Jr.,
by Belchor and Annie Noyes of Salem, Massachusetts, in 1786.
William Daniels, Jr., bringing his wife, followed his father to Roanoke
Island. William Daniels, Jr., inherited the 738 acres from his father
and gave the south half of the Island to his several sons and daughter, who married Tilletts and Midgetts.

Melvin R. Daniels, Dare County Registrar of Deeds for 54 years
prior to his death in 1973, provided the above information to
Josephus Daniels, which he in turn included in his book "The Story of

a Tar Heel Editor." Josephus claimed kinship to Melvin R. Daniels of Manteo. He believed that his great-grandfather had come from Roanoke Island. In their correspondence, Melvin told him about a Daniels house built in Salem, Massachusetts, in 1680, that he had discovered.

If Josephus Daniels was related to the Roanoke Island Daniels, he is probably the most famous and best known descendent of that first Daniels. Josephus served as Secretary of the Navy from 1913 to 1921 and Ambassador to Mexico from 1933 to 1942. Before he became politically active, Josephus had consolidated the *State Chronicle* and *North Carolinian* to form the *Raleigh News and Observer,* and served as its editor until his death in 1948 at 86 years of age.

George Charles Daniels, my mother's father, born February 1, 1849, lived on part of that property in Wanchese on the southern end of Roanoke Island. He fished and farmed and claimed he fathered eighteen children, nine by each of two wives. My mother, Inez Lynn Daniels, was the first child by his second wife Margaret Ann Johnson.

He nearly left the island during the Civil War. Orphaned early, raised by his grandmother, at thirteen he decided to volunteer. He got as far as the gate, where pear trees stood on either side, with his little bundle of clothes before he turned back. "Granny, we don't own slaves. You need me more than they need me as a drummer boy for the Confederacy. I'm not going to leave you."

Margaret Ann Johnson, a single woman with a daughter, Elrado, lived in the Daniels home during the last illness of George's wife Nancy, who died at thirty-six years in 1886. She had birthed nine children. The four unaccounted for may have died in infancy. The two oldest, daughters Lucetta and Arletta, were already married and out of the home by the time Mama was born, March 3, 1890. Girls married very early in those days. Some of their children were Mama's contemporaries. However, there were still little boys of that first family. So Margaret and her daughter Elrado, thankful for food and a roof over their heads, stayed on to help that good man after Nancy's death in 1886. George, thirteen years older, married Margaret sometime before my mother's birth.

My mother loved her father fiercely and was partial to him. She believed Margaret still had feelings for Elrado's father, Zeke Daniels, a relative but not a brother of her father George. She followed at her dad's heels, helping with his chores—feeding the pigs and going to the "cutting sedge" for wood for the fireplace. He called her "Nezie." Sometimes it took him a long time to arrive at her name as he habitually called the names of all his older children before he came to hers. She laughed about that. Another story she enjoyed telling about him concerned a pear.

"Daughter, don't pick that pear. I'm waiting to see how big it will grow." Like Eve in the garden, denial only made his little daughter more anxious to taste that fruit. She climbed the tree and ate the pear. When her father discovered the stem with only a core, he said, "Daughter, my pear!"

"Dad, I didn't pick it!"

Her eyes twinkled as she remembered his laugh when he said, "No, but you sure ate it!"

∽

In the following account, written in 1967, Inez reveals something of her relationship to her father and her observations of customs of church attendance of that day:

It was my good fortune to take trips with George Charles, Senior, to a picnic for a Sunday school. He didn't like to miss one, either at Manns Harbor, Wanchese, or Manteo, on the North End, on the hills or near them.

Sometimes I attended speeches at Manteo in the Court House. I remember one especially well. J.Y Joyner, Superintendent of Public Instruction, was the speaker. George Charles never sat way back. He either wanted to be near the speaker, the better to hear every word that was spoken, or perhaps it was a habit he had acquired from church attendance where he always sat up front in the "Amen

Corner." I never understood why a certain place was for Amen.

The men of mature years occupied the upper left hand corner of the old church at Wanchese. They did say "Amen" occasionally if the discourse was pleasing to their understanding. Now the Amen is seldom given in the Methodist Church. We have just as good, perhaps better, preaching now than in the yesteryears of which I reminisce. But styles or habits change in everything else from dress to houses, so why not style of showing appreciation?

I can look back over the years and I seem to hear a lot of those old "Ameners" giving, "Amazing Grace, how sweet the sound..." all the power of their lungs. They did put in a lot of grace notes where they were not written in the music, but they really had rhythm and gusto, if they lacked time and strict adherence to the tempo. I often wondered why the ladies sat in the middle or on the right hand side away from their men folks. It was a rare thing to see men and women go in church and sit together.

Their second child, Sara Montez, born May 31, 1891, died five days later. Lillian was born December 30, 1892. When old enough, she and Inez assumed much responsibility for their younger siblings, helping one another with their care.[11]

My mother and her sisters Elrado (Rado) and Lillian sewed. Early in their lives, one or the other of them would be invited to go to a home and stay there for a period of time to sew for that family. Children always needed to have their outgrown clothes replaced. In this way, they made a little money and were fed and housed. This helped the economics at their own home.

Dr. Gates, a Manteo physician and widower engaged to Rado, encouraged my mother to go away to school. Wanchese offered only the basic education of that time. Perhaps he believed the claim of some person who read the knots on her head and determined Inez had potential. Mama, with five dollars he gave her, two blouses, and one skirt, enrolled at North Carolina Normal School in Greensboro in

1910. She worked out her tuition costs in the dining hall. After only one year, her mother Margaret's health made it necessary for her return home to help the family.

Long before her death, Rado gave Lillian's daughter Myrt the engagement ring that Dr. Gates had given her. A misunderstanding between Rado and Dr. Gates caused a breach in their relationship. He died before their differences could be resolved; and Rado, eleven years older than Inez, went to Berkley, Virginia, to make her living by dress making and renting rooms in her rented home.

Berkley is no longer named as part of the Norfolk area. It seems to me that Chesapeake now encompasses what used to be Berkley and South Norfolk.

I enjoyed my visits with Aunt Rado each summer. She was an attractive woman. Once I asked why she never married. She told me about her engagement but did not give it as a reason for not having married. Instead she said, "If I had married I would have been expected to have children. Children ache your arms when they are little and your heart when they are grown."

A less serious answer she gave with a chuckle was, "I couldn't marry them all! So I didn't marry any of them."

A man, who roomed at her home for several years until his sister came to live with him, may have been a boyfriend. His name was Guy Ireland. I adored him like another uncle. When he came in from duty on the Coast Guard cutter he captained, he spoiled us by taking us for a soda pop at a drive-in over in Brambleton. Aunt Rado spoiled me too. She would promise that when she got her work caught up, we would take the trolley to Ocean View Amusement Park to spend a whole day. We walked over the Berkley Bridge to Monticello Avenue, instead of boarding the trolley in Berkley, in order to save a nickel.

Even as a child, I was aware that Aunt Rado had a hard time financially, and I did not make demands that would be a hardship for her. A special, generous person, she was an important part of my life. Every niece who would accept her hospitality was welcomed. While she had a reputation for being hard to get along with, all knew that her home was open and welcoming to her friends and kinfolks.

She taught me to drink coffee, to crochet, and not to pay a tradesman until the work was completed. I loved her dearly.

When she was old and no longer able to maintain herself, she lived in a nursing home in Manteo for a while. On one visit I made, she told me about lending her shoes to a beau to go to a dance. When she got confused, she said, "Sybil, don't lose your mind when you get old."

Aunt Lillian took responsibility for her care when she could no longer live there. By then she was bedridden. I taped a conversation one day when she was talking about the pretty dresses she once had. Lillian agreed, "Just as pretty as anyone's..."[12]

Years after husband Nathan's death, Lillian married Arthur Williams, a widower, and they lived out their lives together. He died first, and Lillian died January 20, 1985.

While Mama did not make sewing her livelihood, she did lots of it during her lifetime. Instead, she took the Dare County Board of Education examination, passed it, and received a certificate to teach school. She taught her first year in Ahoskie, North Carolina. In Dare County, arriving by mail boat and while living with Minerva Whidbee and spouse, she taught in a one-room schoolhouse in Trent, now Frisco, on Hatteras Island. Trent, at that time quite small, is situated four or five miles north of Hatteras Village.

And so it was that Andrew would hitch Old Deck to the cart and make that trip to Trent to court Inez. I have no idea how often, but knowing young love's fervency and the determination of the man who became my father, I expect frequently. Perhaps another young man of Hatteras courted a girl in Trent and made the trip with him. Cart and horse, sand ruts, weather, and mosquitoes made it difficult in daylight. It had to be especially arduous and lonely on a moonless night. Maybe he timed his visits by the moon!

He told a story about coming home one moonlit night and being scared out of his wits by an apparition. He approached the village and the road that snaked around before crossing The Slash Bridge and into the village. He had to pass the dipping vat, which was abreast of where Atlantic View Hotel would be built in years to come. The dipping vat, a cement trough through which cattle and horses were driven, contained some mixture to help protect them from insects. It stood on a knoll, and it was there by it that he saw his specter, a woman with her long hair blowing in the wind. Old Deck went sedately by the place, and the next day Daddy discovered that his woman was nothing more than a small, gnarled oak tree on the brow of the hill.

Mama and Daddy were married December 9, 1914, and went to live with his parents and all those others in the Austin home. Less than a month before their first child, Andrew Shanklin, Jr., arrived, Mama's mother Margaret died, November 30, 1915. Shank was born December 26, 1915.

In 1922, after their marriage and three children, Mama taught at Hatteras, the largest village on the Island, for three years. There were more children and another teacher to teach them. An account of her experience follows:

> Two teachers taught seven grades. One had from the six-year group through the ten-year group. Now we call those groups grades, one through the fourth. The other teacher had the rest of the children, eleven to sixteen years.
>
> One never got as far as high school. But how well some of those fourteen, fifteen and sixteen year olds knew their books! They should, of course, for sometimes one did one book over two or three times.
>
> Pretty much the same was true with the first four years of work. Repeat and repeat was the order of the educational system. I thought I would never leave the big geography and big history behind, or any of the other subjects for that matter.
>
> Folks know a lot more about sanitation than was so in the Then period. The toilet facilities were nil. No one had to wash hands after restroom visits. The only water available was a

wooden water bucket brought at the beginning of school. A tin dipper was the common property of all. All drank and dipped and readapted for the cooling draught with never a thought of a germ. In fact, I cannot recall that the word germ was given much credence then.

The outhouse was a two or three holer for the girls—the same for the boys—over open ground. That was before the days of pits. The neighbor's hogs usually did a clean up job each night.

Josephine, their third child, was delivered January 25, 1921, by Leah Ballance, a midwife. Jeanette Stowe was another midwife in the village. January 10, 1926, Maurice Bernard Folb, a naval pharmacist mate, with the help of his wife Sybil Miller, a Buxton girl he married, delivered Sybil Bernadine. My name honors both of them.

Many other babies received his name during the time he and several midwives helped, while Hatteras Island was without a medical doctor. He traveled the length and breadth of the island, isolated from the mainland by water, accessible only by boat.

Before the automobile arrived, ferries did not even run across Hatteras and Oregon inlets. Islanders wanting to travel to upper Dare County and beyond relied on the mail boat or fishing boats. Always seeking to satisfy my desire to see more of the world, I once sailed from Hatteras to Wanchese on an oil boat to visit relatives. The captain of the boat was probably related to Mama.

About three years after my birth, Mama had a gall bladder operation in St Vincent Hospital in Norfolk. Before the operation, her doctor told Mama that she would probably not keep her baby. She did not know she was pregnant. But in her feisty way, knowing her father would pray for her and believing in the Father who answers prayers, she said, "I bet I will!"

Blood poisoning or septicemia threatened her life, and she thinks the doctors gave her up for dead. Before antibiotics had been discovered, she won her bet. She lived.

However, when Daddy had received the dire predictions from the doctor, he decided he should take his children to tell their mother good-bye. Daddy owned a car by 1929. He called ahead to have a ferry come and pick us up on the south side of Oregon Inlet. Since it was dark, the captain of the ferry would not be able to see the flag travelers usually hoisted to alert him to come across for us. There was too little traffic to warrant regular service.

I have some memory of that trip, although I was not more than three. I awoke and asked Margie where we were, and she said we were in Kill Devil Hill. That made me afraid that the devil might get us. Later, I told them why I was afraid. The name sounded to me like "Kill Devil Me."

In spite of neglect by nurses and predictions of her doctor, Mama lived to see the birth, November 12, 1930, of beautiful baby girl Cecelia Ramona. Mama always said, "After the five year break between Jo and Sybil, Mona and Sybil seemed like a second family."

For sure, when we arrived, our parents had become experienced and wise. Mama loved all children, those of other mothers as well as her own.

Some years later Daddy had his first heart attack. His diagnosis was congestive heart failure. One fearful, tearful night, he told Mama he was afraid their children would be orphaned. The doctors had told him that Mama might not live more than a couple of years. Unable to console him by usual means, she confronted him with the facts. She had lived to have the baby the doctors did not think she would carry to term. Baby Mona was several years old. She told him that if he died, she would take care of their five children. The truth helped more than her sympathy. Both lived beyond the promised three score and ten years.

Mama said she had wanted a dozen sons. She changed her mind, confessing that her one son caused her more anguish then her four daughters. She said, "First children should be born last."

She seemed to feel she had failed to be all she should be as a mother. However, echoing her sentiment and having had the experience of three sons who did not always make decisions that were beneficial to them, I know loving mothers do the best they know how to do, making mistakes and learning by them. Mothers cannot make choices for their grown children, who are responsible for their choices, their consequences, and their happiness. Her devotion paid off in all of our lives and many other lives besides. Inez fit the description of an ideal wife of Proverbs 31: 10-31. Her husband could trust in her, and her children do praise her.

Chapter 8
Life as Usual, Except...
❧

*L*ife seemed better in some ways for Hatteras Island than it had been before the Great Depression. Government decisions made during that time actually helped an area where the economy, dependent on fishing, already knew depression.

After a trip to California in 1936, my father purchased a station wagon. He planned to take our immediate family on that trip the following year. Well, we never got to make that trip. I overheard something about that being due to "the depression." At ten years, I did not know what they might mean, only that Daddy could not keep his promise to us. We never did make that trip to California as a family.

The worst economic period in United States history was between 1930 and 1940. I read in a resource book: "Depression Generation will be ages 65 or older." I fall in that age group. But it would take a history buff, versed in economics, to explain all the factors that caused it and the factors responsible for our nation's recovery. I am neither.

Daddy said people in our area felt the effects later than those in other areas. As a little girl, I trusted my intelligent father, who read the newspaper and listened to the radio.

As an adult, with some knowledge of economics acquired while I was a pharmacy student at Carolina and garnered from living my life, I now understand that when people on the mainland had less and less money to buy fish, the price of fish went down and the demand for fish became depressed. Then our area began to feel the effects of the stock market crashing that eventful day of October 24, 1929.

As I review those years, I expect the Great Depression accounts for gifts acquired with coupons for our Christmas gifts at some point and for my mother sewing doll clothes for all our dolls one year—a most memorable gift and a cherished memory for me, nevertheless.

Naturally, my father was affected in several ways. His nets brought less return, his freight boat carried fewer fish to market, and the fishermen who depended on credit from local merchants for food and other necessities had less money to keep their bills paid monthly in his store.

As a little girl, I observed there were many new young men on our island. They lived in a camp in Buxton with their superintendent, Mr. Byron. He directed their work of erecting sand fences and planting sea oats on our sandy beach to rebuild the shores. Never mind that it took away sand from the shore to cover those fences and build the dunes. Those dunes were leveled in 1936 when a mighty hurricane brought water in from the Pamlico Sound deeper than we had ever seen a tide. Many blamed those "d—— sand fences" for keeping the water trapped, for not allowing the tide to flow over the island, unhampered, from the Pamlico to the Atlantic Ocean as it had prior to their erection.

Older girls dated the boys. Some married the girls and became a part of our community. Leonard Gillikin married Neva Stowe.

The Civilian Conservation Corps helped a great many young men, some of them our own. Daniel Willis, who owns a dock at Hatteras, joined. Edward Midgett of Buxton, now deceased, another area businessman, served in the CCC for a number of years, along with many others. Anyway, more money floated around from their thirty-dollar-a-month checks than was usual for the area.

While the CCC boys were young, between 17 and 23, and unmarried, the group that came later seemed older, and some were married. Their camp was in Trent (later renamed Frisco) woods. Research reveals to me that these men were part of a relief program administered by the Works Project Administration begun in 1935. Men and women who benefited were known to us as WPA workers. Critics among us used to call road workers "shovel leaners," an unkind judgment and probably a bad evaluation of what was happening as they worked to improve roads and did other needed tasks. Some men from Hatteras and six other island villages joined the WPA, too.

One project of the WPA was to provide outdoor toilets with pits. Our back yard bloomed with new pine ones having two holes. Our old one had three: one for Daddy Bear, one for Mama Bear, and one for wee Baby Bear. I never remember being there with Mama and Daddy. But one birthday I had appropriated it to play Post Office until Mama called me to the back door to find out why a little boy and a little girl had gone in together. Her reaction was an emphatic, "No, Sybil!"

Some of the WPA men, as well as the CCC boys, found wives among local women. Scottie Gibson, who married Nettie Robinson, became a successful businessman and eventually bought Atlantic View Hotel. For years he and Nettie did most of the hard work involved in that operation. Willie Newsome married Nora Stowe, daughter of Nora Stowe. He prospered, too, as a Hatteras businessman.

Everyone owned his or her home debt free. That station wagon? Chances are that my father paid cash for it. People there lived that way. There were no mortgages. Storeowners, like my father, were ones to whom they were indebted. I am sure most debtors hated a debt as much as my father did. They worked hard for what they earned and were suspicious of government handouts and these strange young men who benefited from programs Franklin D. Roosevelt, that man up in the White House, had provided under something called the New Deal. And the Second New Deal! Even Social Security, begun around 1935 and 1936, came under their suspicion, deemed "another handout" and a threat to one's self- respect and pride.

One program under Social Security provided welfare grants for local distribution and included aid to dependent children. How merciful that must have been for widowed women with young children! There were several in Hatteras village who benefited from that welfare grant section of Social Security. In years since, there have been billions who have received aid.

One innovation I enjoyed and appreciated was school lunches, which I sometimes enjoyed, even though our home was just across the road from the school and I was not considered one of the needy. I never remember seeing pinto beans before that. The only ones in Daddy's store were the big white lima beans, black-eyed peas, and navy beans.

Mrs. Theresa Rollinson, whose name is on my birth certificate as a notary public, cooked for the lunch room, located in the back west room of the old school, where I had attended first grade. Later, Lucy Peele cooked, too. Cabbage, biscuits, beef stew, those pinto beans, and corn bread were so good and satisfying to my curious appetite when I stayed to buy my lunch. Opportunities to work and earn instead of being forever at the mercy of chance and charity helped many men and women among us.

Women like Nora Stowe and Vera Robinson were paid to go into homes to help with children or the ill. Some made mattresses over at the schoolhouse and/or sewed dresses for needy folks. The village buzzed with activity.

Also, the first library was set up in Hatteras School under that program. Vera Robinson took care of the library. Her husband had drowned, leaving her with the responsibility for her son Marvin and her mother, Mrs. Jean Scott.

That summer, I determined to read all the books in the library. As limited as the library must have been and as few volumes as it must have contained, I failed to read them all. I took "The Adventures of Robin Hood" with me when I went to visit my cousin in Wanchese. I spent many hours trying to get through that very large book. I will never forget Gene Stratton Porter's "A Girl of the Limberlost." Maybe that was all I managed that summer. No, I think I did better than that, for Mrs. Vera was a great encourager. Having a monthly income, no matter how small, rather than depending on making pongee dresses for some little girl whose parents could afford to pay her, must have been a blessed relief to her. I can only guess. I was too young to be her confidante.

Another great improvement happened around this time. Tom Eaton came from Winston Salem and built a gray, corrugated-metal-covered building on the docks, which provided electricity and ice for the community. Eaton put up the money. Frazier Peele, married to Viola Willis, put up the land, which was situated behind their home. That property had belonged to Viola's father, Irish Willis.

Herbert Oden and Cecil Ballance helped wire houses and Herman Burrus managed the office for Eaton and Peele. Later, when the Rural Electrification Association brought electricity to the island, Herbert Peele joined them and acted as their manager for eleven years. When Maurice Burrus bought the building for housing Hatteras Texaco Oil Company, Herbert Oden remembers that he bought a twenty-five percent share from Burrus. When Burrus sold to Jim Mullen, Oden retained forty-nine percent. Eventually, the property was sold to Donald Oden, whose family still retains the property.

The "ill wind" that this era most surely seemed for our country and others brought money into our village, money that would not have been there except for the worldwide crisis known as The Great Depression. It brought improvements to our village that were helpful to everyone.

Many European countries had already developed social security programs before World War I. While the New Deal ended in 1937, programs and agencies that were begun then still exist. These changed the relationship between the government and the people. We changed. For a little girl like me, the Great Depression seemed not so bad, except I had to be much older before I could afford to visit California.[13]

This piece has appeared previously in *The Island Breeze* and in *A Generation Speaks: Voices of the Great Depression* (2000).

Chapter 9
Hatteras Child's Christmas

❦

Christmas is an awesome time for a child, conditioned by family and peers, as well as the unexplainable, to expect wonderful things to happen. In Hatteras, where I grew up during the thirties in the midst of a worldwide crisis known as The Great Depression, our Christmas Eve program at Hatteras Methodist Church was the most important event. For my siblings and me, activity and changes in our father's store ran a close second.

Turkey and plum pudding were not the fare we expected. We were fortunate to have a goose as the main attraction at Christmas dinner, with rutabagas, sweet potatoes, collard greens or cabbage, and the usual pies and cakes. One we called "Poor Man's Cake," * made without some usual ingredients and full of raisins, may have been a substitute for fruitcake. "Pone bread,"** a heavy bread made with corn meal and molasses and soured before baking, was very popular in some homes. And I never knew how turkey tasted until Mama decided to raise her own.

She acquired a tom and hen from somewhere and began her experimentation. Mama enjoyed new challenges. (Later she had Rev. Bill Parkin bring her a piglet to raise and honored our pastor by naming said pig Bill.) Tom turkey grew into a large, ill-tempered bird. Once he caught my bare feet with his sharp talons as I crossed the walk from washhouse to our back door. I avoided him, afraid of his assaults. He attacked Daddy walking in the yard. He flew up onto his back, beating Daddy with his powerful wings.

"Get! Get you crazy bird!" Daddy cried, flailing his arms. "GET OUT OF HERE!"

That turkey even went across the road to Mr. Dolph Burrus' store to take on Mr. Dolph, who had a home in Buxton, as he got out of his truck one morning. Mr. Dolph was a competitor for grocery business, but the rivalry between my father and him was friendly. Tom made his attack without any human authority. Tom was a foul fowl.

When Mama sacrificed him for Christmas dinner, I felt no regret. Not until later, that is. I ate turkey and too much rich chocolate candy sent to the family by Mr. Henry Massoletti, a restaurant owner from New York City, who owned a cottage at Hatteras. I became very ill. For years I told anyone offering me turkey, "I'm allergic to turkey. It makes me sick."

Community life revolved around family, church, and school. Both Hatteras School and Hatteras Methodist Church were across the sandy road from our house. I loved the old church of my childhood, where in the summer, hot and uncomfortable, we fought mosquitoes; sometimes I allowed one a good meal before swatting it, splattering blood on my forearm. Revivals lasted two weeks.

I loved it in the winter when we huddled near the shiny, old brown Heatrola, which housed a black, cast iron body that had to have coal from the coal bin at the back of the church. Best of all I loved it at Christmastime.

Our school principal read us the Christmas story from the Bible—we had chapel once a week—and told us stories to inspire us to work hard and not give up, to be like the frog in the milk that kicked and kicked until it could climb up onto a block of butter, safe from drowning.

Of course, we read and sang about the Christmas story in Sunday school. We drew names and exchanged small gifts among our classmates at school and at church school. Our mothers saw that we were provided with gifts for our teachers.

Preparation for the church Christmas Eve program took most of our attention and after-school time as Christmas approached. I do not remember if we celebrated Advent, starting four Sundays before Christmas. I do remember enactment of the story about the Nativity and Holy Family, because we wondered which village baby would be chosen to play Baby Jesus. Our main concerns were to learn our songs and speeches.

Daddy's store became a place of mystery and surprises as Christmas approached. Packages arrived on the freight boat, Cathleen, from Elizabeth City, from Butler Brothers, that far away place named Baltimore, Maryland, as well as the wholesale houses in Elizabeth City.

Shortly before Christmas those boxes would be opened after the store had closed for the night. By next morning, exciting new things had taken the place of regular merchandise on the shelves. Mona and I found it hard not to touch every item. Our young hearts were greedy. Dark cobalt blue bottles of Evening in Paris tempted us, not only to touch but also to sniff. The two showcases on the dry goods side of the store were filled with sets of Evening in Paris and other kinds of cosmetic sets for both men and women. The shelves that usually held bolts of cloth, bulk socks, and a bit of lingerie (panties specifically) now held boxed handkerchiefs, socks, ties, and a few toys—things to see and admire.

On the far side, the grocery side, a wooden bucket of mincemeat sat on the counter with a large metal container of shredded coconut. Beneath that counter, large boxes contained pecans, almonds, nigger toes (I never knew them as Brazil nuts as a child), and English walnuts. Stored there with the nuts were heavy, sectioned, cardboard boxes containing chocolate covered nougat, cherries, and Brazil nuts and peach blossom candy. Delightful to our eyes and noses, we were as tempted as Eve in the Garden of Eden. Our desire for sweets, hers for knowledge of good and evil, caused us to disobey the authority in our lives. We ate far more candy than we were given, or Daddy knew.

Speeches were distributed at the first practice meeting at church before school recessed for Christmas. It seemed further ahead than it probably was. We met several times after school at the white, clapboard Methodist Church next door to our school to learn and practice the songs and our speeches with the older lady volunteers, who offered their time and patience for us.

Old tradition, rather than busy Christmas activity, kept us from getting our tree and putting it up early. We waited until Christmas Eve. That tradition came from the old country, like the celebration of Old Christmas on January 5th at Rodanthe on the northern end of the Island, when they roasted oysters and greeted Old Buck. We did not take the tree down until after Epiphany, Old Christmas. The old belief was that Santa Claus came on Christmas Eve to bring gifts and trim the Christmas trees as well. Poor Santa!

The last practice came on the afternoon of the day before the performance on Christmas Eve. Some men of the church had found a big cedar tree in Buxton or Trent and had stood it up in front of the dark, varnished, diagonal sheathing in the left chancel area of the church by the time of our last practice. Our excitement made practice noisy and difficult for our prompters.

Gifts we gave and received were neither plentiful nor expensive. Mama saved coupons to order gifts. Octagon Soap helped make clothes clean with boiling and scrubbing on a washboard. Octagon coupons bought good premiums.

While we hoped to keep our gifts secret, we searched for hiding places for gifts to us from others. Sometimes we found hiding places, not meaning to find them, spoiling our surprises. Strangely, it did not stop us from searching. Such contradiction!

Mona and I pooled our money saved from our earnings. Mama paid us a dollar a week to help at home. We did not have allowances as such. We were given what we needed. Mama felt it would encourage our cooperation if we received money and learned to save it for what we might want that was not provided for us. Money in hand, we went down the road to Mr. Dan Oden's store to do our shopping. He was very patient with two small girls as we tried to decide. Helpful, too. He made suggestions to fit our resources.

We expected new clothing at Christmas and Easter. New clothes were not considered gifts, but we five children appreciated that they were part of our Christmas. I loved the cards that came to Mama and Daddy each year. I read every one and followed the lives of families they heard from every year.

Mothers who sewed had been stitching new clothes for weeks. Mrs. Jean Austin had the remarkable ability of being able to take a dress that fitted, look at a picture of the dress desired in Sears, Roebuck or Montgomery Ward, and create that dress from the material given to her. She and Eleanor Stowe, swamped with material and dreams, were driven by holiday deadline. Mrs. Vera Robinson made a lovely beige pongee dress for me once. But most of the time Mama sewed for us.

One Christmas, Mama used her creative ability and skill with the needle to make new dresses for dolls belonging to my younger sister, Mona, and me. My prettiest one, made from a scrap of material, was pale, pink chiffon with tiny buttons on its gathered yoke. My favorite doll, Twinkle Toes, had a pretty one, too. By Christmas morning, every doll had a new dress made from material from other sewing projects that Mama had saved.

Worn shoes had to be replaced. Orders had been sent to Montgomery Ward, Sears, Roebuck, and Spiegel. People crowded the small front entrance of the maroon-painted post office, a short distance from Rollinson Creek landing where the mail boat came when it arrived from Manteo, via other villages on Hatteras Island. Waiting for Miss Maude O'Neal, the postmaster, to sort the mail, packages last, caused anxiety to mount in us! Would the big, fat bags of mail contain our shoes, dresses, and gifts?

When my shoes arrived from Montgomery Ward one year, I had two right shoes that did not even match—a catastrophe. I had been chosen to lead the procession from the back of the church in the annual Christmas Eve program. It seemed very important that I look right in every way.

It was too late to reorder shoes that I needed very badly. Mama could not make shoes from the scraps in her sewing basket. I had a crisis. How could I lead the procession in worn-out shoes that two coats of polish did not improve? Mama had tried to console me. Those shoes never had fit, were run down at the heels, and the sole had become loose. Mama tried glue for that. That did not work either.

"I'm not going to walk in the front of the line in those shoes!" I cried in frustration, angry at those careless people at Montgomery Ward Catalogue Department.

Mama put her arms around me and tried to reassure me. I was inconsolable. My heart ached. I thought of revolt. As much as I wanted everyone to see my beautiful brown dress, I was ready to "cut off my nose to spite my face." I would not be in the program at all. I just did not care if everyone else felt as disappointed as I did. I hoped they would, in fact.

Later Mama found me nursing my insult. She held a pair of green suede shoes in her hand—Jo's shoes. "Sybil, Jo says you can wear her new shoes."

Glowering, I looked at those shoes suspiciously. Well, I had never worn a pair of suede shoes. Mama stood there holding them, waiting for my decision. They had a small heel on them. I began to think they might do. I would look pretty grown up with them and silk hose, wouldn't I?

"Okay!" I said, reluctant to let go my sulk. Oh, but I was so relieved. I would not have to give up my position at the front of the line, after all. I knew my part perfectly. Won't those green suede shoes be something with my new dress, I dreamed.

And then, there I was, all dressed up, standing at the back of the church in the cold bell room, where Mr. Rob Gaskins rang the bell fifteen minutes before Sunday School, again for Sunday School to begin, and again for worship. Shivering with cold and excitement, we waited for the music to start and for Mrs. Rosa Gray, the church school superintendent, to open the door so I could walk proudly at the front of the line. The shoes were too large and had cotton in the toes. But, there I was with those green suede shoes leading the procession.

There were speeches and carols. Under the large cedar tree in the left hand corner of the chancel were bright packages. After the program, someone dressed like Santa Claus gave the gifts to their owners. Each child received a bag of candy and nuts. Then we hurried home, got ready for bed and while we waited for sleep to overcome our excited anticipation, we watched, trying to catch a glimpse of the real Santa Claus. As in other years, we did not succeed, but it was fine, because next morning we found the surprises he had left us. Mama's borrowed stockings bulged with an orange in the toe, English walnuts, nigger toes, hard candy, and chocolates. Christmas Day had arrived at last!

*Poor Man's Cake or Hatteras Cake

Sift together: 4 cups flour, 1 tablespoon baking powder, 2 teaspoonfuls of nutmeg, 2 teaspoonfuls cinnamon.

Raisins—whole package in enough water to cover. Cook and save juice for batter.

Puree cooked raisins. Add one cup shortening, 2 cups sugar, 1 teaspoonful salt and mix all together and bake at 300 degrees in a greased pan of suitable size for 50-60 minutes.

Mix together 1/2 package of confectioner's sugar, butter and additional cinnamon, to taste

** *Hatteras Island Pone Bread*

5c. white corn meal	4 c. hot water
1 cup sifted flour	1 cup cold water
6 tablespoons of sugar	2 tablespoons of shortening
3 tablespoons of molasses	1 1/2 teaspoons salt

Place meal and molasses into bowl and add hot water. Stir well. Add sugar, salt and cold water. Add flours and mix well. Cover for a few hours or overnight. Melt shortening in 2-quart pan, pour in mixture and bake, covered, at 350 F 11/2 hours. Let stand until cool. Cut in squares like corn bread.

This piece has appeared previously in *The Island Breeze* and *Our State* magazine.

Chapter 10
Traveling Hatteras Sands

&

*O*ne morning in Chapel Hill my second husband, Charles
Andre Fetterroll, came home with a story about a man he had
met at the barbershop. I may never meet that man, but he
holds in his mind a memory I share.

Beauty parlors and barbershops are great places for the easy
geniality these places promote among strangers. When we take our
hair down, put it up, or have it cut off, camaraderie seems to flourish.

In the barbershop that morning, my husband had caught up on political opinions and brushed up on economic indicators. He had congrat-
ulated himself on having found a five-dollar haircut in a town that easily asked eight, ten, or more. And a storyteller who amused him with
an oral account of an automobile ride down the sandy roads to the
lower end of Hatteras Island before the highway department established Route 12 beyond Oregon Inlet. With the motion of his body, the
rhythmic rocking of his head, the storyteller described an unforget-
table experience that had happened to him thirty years earlier.

Since Hatteras will always be "home" for me, even though I have
not lived there since 1958, I could visualize more than the entertain-
er. We had shared a common experience. I loved that man as I began
to recall.

Mr. Walter Gaskill was a "drummer" down Hatteras way. Today drummers are called salesmen, or sales representatives, or "detailers." I forget which company employed Walter to drum. However, I do remember a ride with him up that beach in his truck, as I remember many other trips over the sand and ruts.

Mr. Walter was from Wanchese, the village on the southern end of Roanoke Island, where my own mother had been born and raised. I believe Mr. Walter was a cousin of some degree. In any case, Mama felt perfectly comfortable trusting her next to youngest with him for the trip to Wanchese to visit her sister and other relatives.

People did less traveling in those days. Travel was difficult. One ancient aunt of my father never left Hatteras in all her 95 or more years. "Never wanted to," she said.

Not so me! Every chance I could see, I would beg to go visit my relatives up the beach. Walter Gaskill was a means for me that time.

Dressed in a white shirt and tie with no coat, he wore a felt hat. He was a pleasant companion for the ride. As he drove between the sand ruts, our bodies twisted and bumped up and down. He would encourage me with a chuckle, "Hold everything you've got!"

Truth is, you wondered if something might come unhinged or disconnect. It is a wonder that battery cables stayed in place or tires on their rims.

At Oregon Inlet we caught the ferry. Toby Tillett, the captain, was another Wanchese friend and probably kin. His sunny smile welcomed anyone who would join him in the pilothouse for the run across the water separating Nags Head Beach and Hatteras Island. His blue eyes, beneath the soft cap that he wore, were merry. His conversation was easy. For a little ten-year-old girl or a bit more, it was pleasant to be where he was, to enjoy his talk, and listen to the others. A good experience. Peaceful! Safe!

Ten miles north, we came to Whalebone and a filling station run by the family of Elsworth Midgette and called Whalebone. Before the pavement, it was necessary for Mr. Walter to "fill" his tires with air, and sometimes his tank needed gas at Whalebone.

Well, Whalebone actually had whalebones then. As a child, I admired their stark whiteness, never thinking to ask why they happened to be displayed at the left side of the business. These Midgettes were the only people I knew who had any whalebones. I may have questioned in my child's imagination if that was how Mr. Elsworth lost his arm—or was it his leg?

Whalebone is still a place, but that filling station and the whalebones are gone. I doubt I would recognize the location without the name being prominent there on a marker. No need to stop to take air out of automobile tires to travel the sand ruts to get to Hatteras. Gone is Toby's cabin near the Nags Head edge of Oregon Inlet. In its place is a marina filled with beautiful white fishing boats. Nearby is a camping area of the Cape Hatteras National Seashore Park. Spanning Oregon Inlet is the graceful Bonner Bridge, with Hatteras only fifty pavement miles away.

This piece has appeared previously in *The State* (now *Our State*).

Chapter 11
Saturday Ice Cream

❧

*T*oday I can eat ice cream anytime I choose. I can disregard
warnings about calories and cholesterol, take a quick trip to
the freezer section of my grocery store, choose the flavor I like
from a wide variety, and eat my favorite dessert whenever I want. I
can even have two helpings.

None I eat tastes as good as the cones I enjoyed on a Saturday
afternoon when I was a little girl at Hatteras during the thirties.
After I had taken my Saturday bath in preparation for Sunday and
put on a clean dress, Mama or Daddy would give me a nickel to buy
ice cream at Damon Gray's barber shop. Mr. Damon's wife Rosa
mixed up a five-gallon freezer of ice cream each week. My father's
generation depended on Tom Angell, while mine depended on Mr.
Damon and Mrs. Rosa. They were our ice cream angels.

Mr. Damon loaded the freezer into his truck and took it to the fish
house where ice was available to freeze it. Local boys were persuaded to turn the handle for a nickel and a chance to lick the "backbone"
(the clapper). Mrs. Rosa removed it, according to one of those boys, so
they may have had to follow Mr. Damon home to receive their treat.

When the news got out that Mrs. Rosa had made ice cream that
morning, we did not care what the flavor might be. I would have

eaten peach, which I liked least well. A cousin of mine told about having worked all morning for a village man to make a quarter and buying five cones from Mr. Damon that afternoon.

In the small village, Mr. Damon was the only barber and the only undertaker. After Mr. Rob Gaskins, Mrs. Rosa's dad, died, Mr. Damon had the responsibility of ringing the Hatteras Methodist Church (not yet United Methodist) bell to let the people know someone had died. Each toll of the bell represented one year of the deceased person's life. When the bell began to toll, we children began to count, trying to guess who might have died by the knowledge we had of illnesses among the residents. Mr. Damon also delivered freight packages and articles that arrived by freight boat and were too large and heavy for the Postal Service. Once my family relied on him for a distasteful service, the shooting of our dog, which had distemper.

Mrs. Rosa did more than make ice cream, too. She served the church and community as a leader for all the years she lived. I am indebted to her for taking the trouble to compliment my performance in a church play at Hatteras School. I bore the wooden cross from the back of the school auditorium to the front of the stage, singing, "I am coming to the cross. I am poor and weak and blind." There I knelt in my long, white robe and bowed my head. Afterwards she approached me and said, in her quiet, gentle way, "You did well, Sybil." I was so grateful. She served as church school superintendent for many years.

Sitting on a board across the arms of Mr. Damon's barber chair, I had my first awareness of politics. While he snipped, I studied the photos of Theodore Roosevelt and Woodrow Wilson, displayed in dark stained, carved wooden frames on the wall of the shop. Another first for me in that chair was when Mr. Damon had the unfortunate task of informing my older sister Margie, who had taken me there, that I had a bad infestation of head lice.

I can never forget the head scrubbing Marjorie Hope gave me that afternoon. First she doused my head with kerosene. Then she washed my hair with Palmolive soap and rinsed it with diluted vinegar to remove the soap. Shampoo was still in the future. Then she nearly scalped me with a fine-tooth comb, removing the nits from my hair. There is nothing like the combined odor of Palmolive soap and kerosene. Thanks to Mr. Damon, I was freed of those parasites that very afternoon.

When I was older and began to curl my hair on clipperettes (hair pins), I went to Mr. Damon and asked that he cut my hair in lengths. I was horrified to find that he had cut it straight around, as usual, with or without bangs. I cried. He had failed me. My stubby hair did not lend itself to curling for a while. The back ends were too short to turn.

Nevertheless, I still returned to this gentle, affable man, as most of the other children did. He was a friend, a friend who went to great lengths each Saturday to provide us all with a rare, delectable treat. A nickel was, indeed, a small price to pay for ice cream served with love by Mr. Damon and Mrs. Rosa.

This piece has appeared previously in *The State*.

Chapter 12
Lady Postmaster Swimming Teacher

❦

*T*he alarm jarred me out of sleep. Hurriedly, I jumped to reach the button on the back of the Big Ben clock placed near my bed the night before.

No one stirred as I slipped into my red wool swimsuit and crept downstairs, slowly and deliberately, to avoid the step that creaked. I let myself out the front door, heard the click of the latch as I released the knob, and hoped no one had awakened.

It was barely dawn. I had an appointment with Miss Maude, the postmaster of Hatteras village. I was ten years old in the mid-1930s and not the only young girl sneaking off to meet our informal swimming instructor.

Miss Maude believed in exercise and physical fitness. She told me, when I interviewed her when she was nearly 101 years old, at Highland Farms Rest Home in Black Mountain, North Carolina, August 1986, that as a young woman she had freely walked the seashore in spite of her mother's misgivings. Her mother cautioned that the men at the lifesaving stations would ogle her. Miss Maude dared anyone to question her integrity or virtue. In return, she received the respect she expected. She did as she pleased at a time when women were far less free to come and go as they pleased. I bet she was the first woman at Hatteras to bob her hair.

We children were in awe of our postmaster—note: postmaster. She had taught school before her post office appointment. She let them know that it was to be postmaster. "I was never mistress to anyone," she said.

I tiptoed out of the house, down the steps, and breathed easier when I cleared the gate of our white picket fence. I began to run as soon as my bare feet hit the sand. After crossing the road, I went a short distance to my friend Marian's house, shivering in the damp morning air as I lifted the gate latch of Mr. Dolph Burrus' fence.

Carefully skirting a big live oak with exposed roots, I tapped lightly on the gray cotton screening of Marian's window, whispering her name. Her face appeared, her finger to her lips, beyond the screen. She soon appeared at the back door of their house and joined me in the trek to Miss Maude's house near Rollinson Creek.

Stilling our urge to speak until we got beyond earshot, we crawled through the opening in Marian's family's split-rail fence and crossed the field to the dirt road that led to the post office. We could see Mr. Loran Ballance's Gulf Oil storage tanks beyond. They had a ladder where they could be climbed, and we often had visited the storage tanks on our way to the shallow shoals where we searched for crabs on other days. We hurried along, sometimes tripping over our feet in our haste.

We followed the path through the rushes to Miss Maude's maroon-stained house. There she stood, with her hands on her hips. She wore a black bathing suit and a white bathing cap perched on her head—half on and half off. As we approached, she neither called to us nor spoke. That was okay. We knew she waited for us.

Across her yard in the other direction to our right, we saw other water nymphs like ourselves coming to share our adventure. It must be six o'clock in the morning because we were all ready to go.

Miss Maude loaded as many of us as she could into her little rowboat and rowed us out near the boat locks, halfway down the bridge that led to Mr. Irish Willis' wharf. The water was deep there, up to our armpits or deeper, depending on the tides.

We climbed onto the locks or held onto them as we kicked our feet and strengthened our legs. Sometimes we climbed up and dove from the sturdy six-by-six-inch beams—maybe they were thicker than that. While in the water, we would dig our toes into the hard-packed Pamlico Sound sand to find clams for an early bite, for we had not yet eaten breakfast.

Our austere matron, who handled the mail and took us swimming, fascinated us. During that visit to Black Mountain and our conversation that day, I had the opportunity to make an adult evaluation of the remarkable woman, instead of relying on my limited childhood impressions to define her. More than a century old, she was alert and strong. My sister Mona and I talked with her for more than an hour, as she took us on a trip back in time. She laughed often.

Her father, Urias O'Neal, had been a Yankee soldier and had lost a foot during the Civil War. After the war, he married Jane Willis Burrus, a young widow with two sons, Joseph and Edward. They had a son of their own, who died very young, and five daughters, Carrie, Minerva, Maude, Oma, and Dinah. They taught their daughters at home and fostered in them a spirit of independence. She told us that her father allowed her and her sisters to have boats and to do things his own son might have done.

Miss Maude believed she was her father's daughter in that she held the same opinions he had held. She repeatedly said she had lived her life without regard to the artificial judgments of men, and that she acknowledged only God's authority and judgment.

When a friend once lent her money to attend Littleton Female Institute and said she did not have to repay the loan, Miss Maude would not hear of it. "Paid back every dime!" she declared proudly.

She taught school for several years before seeking the influence of a friend in the Republican Party to help her obtain an appointment in the post office in 1914, before Civil Service. Such positions were political then, awarded to those of the same political sympathies as the administration in office.

That day, Miss Maude expressed her pride in her accomplishments and satisfaction in having acquired "full citizenship" in her lifetime as a woman in government and full rights as a voter in 1923.

She chuckled when we recalled the days of our swim classes. She told us that she had been fascinated by the way the Hatteras children crowded around her. She never married, never had children of her own.

"We are helped by some who never know they helped us," she reflected during our visit. "We, in turn, help others, not always knowing that we have."

Maude O'Neal died October 12, 1987, two months before her 102nd birthday. Her obituary in *The Coastland Times* read:

> "Those who knew Maude O'Neal as a teacher and a postmaster well remember that she feared no one or thing. She was a leader in her village, an independent woman of her time, who fought many good fights in the interest of education and physical fitness. She was instrumental in getting a high school for Hatteras Village in the nineteen twenties after serving as a teacher there since 1907. In 1914 she became postmaster at Hatteras, and in the 1920's she managed both jobs plus the extracurricular activity of teaching swimming to the village children."

As a child, I feared her disfavor and sought to be one invited for her swim excursions. As an adult, I enjoyed her, respected her for who she was, and am grateful for all she did to make my life better. We learned more than we realized from the woman who encouraged us to get up so early to go swim.

This piece has previously appeared in *The Island Breeze* and *The State*.

Chapter 13
Tents, Places of Refuge
❧

My friend Marian called her older brother Bill "Boy," even when he became a man. Our inspiration for our tent-above-all-tents came when we saw his "tent" in a horse stable. He called it a tent. It looked more like a camp.

In our building efforts, we had made less permanent structures of empty burlap bags garnered from Daddy's store. Wooden bins holding new nails were conveniently near the back door of the store, behind one wall of Daddy's office. The bins were about eighteen inches high. I helped myself to a few nails; I did not think he would mind, so I did not ask him.

Once, we made one of those burlap tents with two rooms on top of the cesspool in the middle of the back yard. Why we equipped one room with a bucket for a toilet is a mystery. Our outdoor toilet was not that far away.

Our burlap structures kept out the intense sunlight, but not the rain. (It may have been the location, or it may have been because David Austin, my cousin, decided to use our facility. That may have doomed it. Adults see such things as crises.) Nevertheless, for a season of building, it satisfied our creative, architectural appetites; and for a season of play, we had the satisfaction of accomplishment.

The truck cab someone had propped against our outdoor toilet made the greatest hideaway. Small and private, but big enough for two of us. A friend, or my younger sister Mona, and I could crawl inside. There we had our cache, where the seat of the truck had been. We covered the space with a board and kept our stores safe. Raw potatoes with salt and pepper tasted so good in that snug, private place away from the sun, the rain, and the vigilant eyes of our parents. Burlap sacks draped both openings.

When it disappeared, my sister Mona and I complained loudly and tearfully about the loss of our playhouse. Our brother, ten years older than I, said defensively, " Yes, I took it away. I couldn't even go to the 'outhouse' and have privacy."

We felt our brother quite heartless, that he had overstepped his authority by destroying our place of refuge. We wanted Mama and Daddy to take our side. We did not understand his need for privacy any more than he did ours, I guess. Oh, we enjoyed that place and grieved its loss.

Now, having seen the place Bill and his friends had, my friends and I determined we would build a more permanent structure, a structure that would be all the others had not been. It would be built of wood on the farthest corner of one of the lots belonging to my parents. It would have a roof, and it would be larger than the truck cab.

It helped that O. B. Peele's grandmother's (Martha Oden's) house, next door, had recently undergone partial dismantling. He could provide five posts. We had to have a doorway, you know. We had an eastern exposure, which opened toward the Methodist Parsonage and the Slash beyond. The fifth post placed the doorway on the left front corner of our tent.

Our posts were not all the same length. One of them may have been a fence post. Not able to sacrifice much length, we could not bury them deep enough to make them the same height. We did the best we could, having neither plumb line nor level.

In our haste to complete our dream, we took short cuts, allowing no delays and asking no help. The length of the shortest board determined the dimension of this tent. Starting from the bottom with the peeling, yellow-painted boards, we had to let some jut beyond the posts and other boards. We had no saw. Day after day, we worked to complete our dream.

When we added the section of roof that O. B. had contributed, it sat on the top of the posts at a jaunty angle. It kept out the sun and the rain, even if it failed to add much to the overall expected appearance. We were very fortunate that O. B. found a section of roof from his grandmother's old house intact. If one corner had not dipped due to that shorter post, it would have been fine.

Mama overheard our discussion about adding a stove and discouraged that. We did not have a chimney. She suggested that we cook outside, to avoid smoke and smarting eyes.

On some trash pile we found discarded parts of an old, iron stove body. We placed it on the ground outside, in such a way that air could come from the bottom. Mona and I learned from a very harrowing experience a year or so earlier that fire without air will not burn, even if fed kerosene or gasoline. It was Mona's time to go and get kerosene to help our effort to make a fire in the bottom of a 5-gallon lard can. When she added gasoline she'd pumped from the wrong barrel, the fire blazed into her face. Since it was a cold November day, cold water filled a bucket under the eaves of one of the sheds. Luckily, I quickly plunged Mona's hot face into that icy water. I made a discovery that became common knowledge long after I had forgotten that incident and had children of my own, when we were still using Unguentine for burns. No blisters formed, but she had a very pink face, minus eyebrows and eyelashes. Her front hair had been singed a bit.

Mama, so wise, made me stay with Mona, propped up in their bed. I think I read to her. Perhaps it was penance and served to take care of my guilt. The smell of Noxzema always reminds me of that day.

More Mama wisdom: When a bunch of us playing in the yard got into a disagreement, she gave all of us a dose of cod liver oil, our friends as well as us. It was effective in keeping us congenial. The one thing worse is castor oil. I still think of that day I told Mama I was sick because I did not want to go to school. A dose of castor oil was thought to take care of most childhood illnesses. Never again did I lie about being sick. It did not cure any tummy ache, but it sure cured my lying tongue.

Having begged or appropriated a frying pan from one of our parents, we were finally ready to cook. We built a fire in our "stove." Potatoes, from a parent's kitchen, and eggs, directly from our chickens' nests, cooked out of doors were the best I have ever eaten. For sure!

Years later, watching my next door neighbor build a perfectly symmetrical tree house out of new lumber for his family of boys, I knew he either had the dream himself or had stolen it from one of them. They watched, while he had all the fun. They never even hammered a nail that I saw.

After it had been built, the boys sometimes climbed up the perfect little ladder to sit in the tree house and look around before they crawled back down. It did not hold their interest long, and the builder did not go up and sit in the house to appreciate his creation. I felt sad. Our wonderful habitat had been more dream than reality. But it had kept us involved many happy hours. Remembering our last and finest tent, I am convinced that my journey toward my goals is where I find the real excitement and satisfaction. Reaching my goal is an anticlimax.

This piece has previously appeared in *The Island Breeze.*

Chapter 14
Places of Recreation and Trade

❧

During an earlier generation, the youth of the Island had enjoyed the excitement of sailboat competition. Only once do I remember a sailing experience, and what an experience it turned out to be!

One summer day someone decided it would be fun to go to Trent (Frisco) for a picnic and to pick wild grapes, plentiful on the sand hills at the southern edge of Trent in late July or August. We often walked the four miles for picnics and to play on the hills. Either we would walk the sandy ruts of what we called the "inside road," or we would walk along the surf until we reached Creeds Hill Lifesaving Station, where a great, white water tank invited thirsty walkers to drink, or drivers to replenish dry car radiators.

However, this day the boys had been able to borrow a sailboat. So a bunch of boys and girls sailed from Rollinson Creek that morning, up to the bay beyond Durant Point. We tied the boat somewhere near the edge of Trent Woods and walked to the hills. After eating our lunch, picking grapes, and sliding down the hills, we were again on the water in the small sailboat when a sudden summer squall caught us in the bay.

The brisk breeze caught the sail, threatening to capsize the boat, while heavy rain filled it with water, threatening to dump us into the choppy, rain-pelted bay. Two guys jumped overboard to stabilize the boat, while another struggled to take down the sail. Two of us girls emptied our grapes to use the containers for bailing. We resented that the third one came home from the adventure with her grapes when ours had gone overboard.

Brothers Russell and Ivey Austin lived at the northern end of what we called the Back Road. Their boat was moored beyond their parental home in a creek off the bay. They saw us in distress and came in their gas-run fishing boat to our rescue and to pull the boat and us to safety. Louise Oden, Marcelle Burrus, and I walked home from their dock. Rain soaked, our clothes clinging to our young pre-puberty bodies, we had to walk past all the houses and people along the way. The boys, Dalton Burrus, Maylon Boyd Peele, and Edison Meekins, had to return the boat to Roscoe Willis from whom they had borrowed it.

I have told you about Sunday afternoons at Tom Angell's, which our parents enjoyed. Ruby Austin Burrus remembers her father taking her to Tom's when she was a little girl and having Tom, in his starched white clothes, serve them ice cream from a gazebo in his front yard. He played the old organ, his violin, and sang for them. I remember going once myself and having cake to go with the ice cream.

Tom Angell, the lone black man on the Island, inherited the property in 1912 from Inez Angell, widow of Nelson Angell, lighthouse keeper, who had died in 1887. By verbal agreement with Tom's mother (named Vine), Inez Angell had been allowed to take Tom, only six years of age at the time, to live with them. He lived at Hatteras until his death in 1937.[14]

You already know the role ice cream played in the lives of my generation, and how Rosa and Damon Gray provided ice cream on Saturday afternoons in the summer. And how cousin Nacie Peele worked a whole day for Willie Gaskins for twenty-five cents, which he spent to buy five cones of ice cream at Damon's Barber Shop.

You already know about the business my father Andrew S. Austin started in 1908 cutting hair, then graduating to confections and those delightful ices and milk shakes he made without ice cream.

Stores were always favorite meeting places, even before Daddy built his. Mary Ballance told me about stores that had disappeared before I was old enough to remember them. She said Ben Austin once had a store on the beach, just where I do not know. She lived past ninety. I never knew the Ben Austin, who was father of Ben and Harry. It may have been his store.

Bascom Ballance's weathered gray store, north of Gaskins Cemetery, stood across from the location of Daddy's original business, and where Midgette Brothers have their business and motel now. During my childhood, Mr. Bascom's son Reuben ran the store. Mr. Reuben gave the best money value. He would add an extra Mary Jane, when they were two for a penny, in a bag with a nickel's worth of candy.

Mary Ballance married Cecil, a younger son of Mr. Bascom. Her father Jardella had a store up the main road near where the post office had been when Mr. Ballance acted as postmaster. The mail boat came into a dock near her father W. Jardella Ballance's store. It had been prosperous then. By my time, the store still existed, but it was not thriving.

Mr. Jardella Ballance reminded me of Abe Lincoln. His long legs took him back and forth to the store, which had an unpainted, rough exterior. It had a front door, a back door and one window, as I remember. His mother, Leah Ballance, who had delivered my sister Jo and others, lived across the road.

His son Walter married Juanita Tillett, the daughter of my mother's sister Arletta of Wanchese. Walter and his family lived with Mr. Jardella Ballance, whose wife had died years before. I often visited Anna, Walter and Neat's oldest child, my age, to play dominos, cut paper dolls out of the catalogues, eat her mother's delicious ham bone soup for Sunday dinner, or spend the night and enjoy the hot biscuits and oatmeal Juanita stirred to delightful consistency in the morning. Juanita sometime treated Anna and me, when I would be spending the night, with black walnut flavored candy from that store. However, I felt in awe of Anna's grandfather, who seldom smiled.

Yet this man had fished the Hatteras waters, raised three sons and two daughters, and maintained a neat white home, trimmed with yellow, where I loved to visit. Sometimes on Sunday afternoon, Mama would take us up the road to see Juanita, and we would play games, such as, Mother, May I?, Red Light, Little Sally Water, Drop the Handkerchief, Red Rover, and others in their front yard.

Dolph Burrus married Lucy Stowe, whose father Alonzo Stowe had a successful store, established in 1866. After Mr. Stowe's death, Mr. Dolph became its proprietor. The Red and White Supermarket is in the same location as that store. After William Z, youngest son of Dolph and Lucy, inherited the business, he used a drawing of the original building for advertisements. It looked that way when Mr. Dolph and I conducted our business transactions. He would accept Mama's eggs for candy when I could get one or two before Mama collected them from the chicken nests. Sometimes Austin Store and Burrus' provided an item the other lacked for one of their own customers. I confess that my egg transaction was less than honorable, for I conveniently forgot to ask Mama for the eggs I traded.

Litchfield Gaskill, who married Brittie Oden, Uncle Dock's oldest daughter, owned a store down the road near the shore where Nedo's now is. He and Brittie had no children. Dan Quincy, one of Brittie's brothers, had five children and lived across the road from them. The children loved and were loved by the childless couple in a very special way. I remember Mr. Litchfield vaguely, and attending his funeral, a somber affair where the women sang "Abide With Me" and other hymns, slowly and mournfully. I never wanted to miss a funeral, in spite of the feeling of dread it promoted in my young mind.

Mr. Dan became the proprietor of that store. I did business with him when I was a little girl.

Irish Willis built a new store. I never knew it well. It had not even weathered to gray when it burned one hot summer evening. That same evening John Meekins Store burned to the ground, leaving only a set of steps and a safe. Some think Ben Austin's Store burned that same night. Was there an arsonist in our midst? As far as I know the mystery was never solved.

Lee Robinson's store came later than the thirties. Before he had his own store, he was in and out of Daddy's store often. Virgil Willis, heir of Robinson, has a lovely two-storied building on the site of the John Meekins Store. It is attractive and well stocked with merchandise.

Mr. Elsworth Burrus once had a store. It had been closed before my time. It remains in my memory as a landmark, however. Shank was giving Mama a driving lesson, with a bunch of us in the back seat. Shank instructed Mama to turn into a spot by the store to turn around or to let him take over. Instead of hitting the brake, she ran into the side of the store. Only Mama's pride was damaged, but her resolve to learn to drive was demolished. That incident pretty much ended her efforts, except for the day when she needed to go up to take some sewing to Mrs. Elnora Stowe. No one was available to take her, and she was determined to go. I went with her, but remember the jerks and starts and my feeling of anxiety. We made it there and back, however. Mama even cranked that vehicle so it would run.

Mr. Elsworth and Leona (Lone) Austin Burrus had Harry Austin and Henry Gaskill build The Pavillion in 1927, and the Atlantic View Hotel a year later on land acquired from Victoria (Vide) Styron. The Pavillion provided opportunities for entertainment, and Atlantic View was Hatteras Island's first hotel.

The Pavillion, a large square building with a hip roof and windows on two sides, provided a place for movies—at first silent ones. But in 1927 Warner Brothers produced the first "talkie," The Jazz Singer, starring Al Jolson, and Hatteras soon was showing "talkies" too. By 1928 Corlette Burrus, the Burruses' only son, had returned from his years of schooling off the Island and was available to help them manage both businesses.

Snowden Holland, from Chicago, married Lily Peele Stowe, widow of Richard Stowe. The carnival he provided for the community, held in the old Woodmen of the World Lodge on the site of Twiford Funeral Home, was a first and was never repeated. It was Holland who helped install projection equipment at The Pavillion and taught Corlette Burrus how to run the projector to entertain all the young and old of the community.

Actually, older people frowned on movies and mistrusted their morality. Children and others had fewer reservations and more curiosity. Jackie Cooper starred in the first movie I saw. Ruby Austin Burrus and I remember that we wept, but not why. I suspect it was that timeless movie in which someone sang, "Climb upon my knee, Sonny Boy. / You are only three, Sonny Boy…". That song reflects the grief of a father after the little boy has died. Yes, we would have been very sympathetic and tearful.

After film showing, chairs were folded and stacked away, and dancing began on the rough, unpainted floor of The Pavillion. Snacks could be bought at the counter to the right of the dance floor.

Later when The Pavillion had been moved away from the front of the hotel and closer to the Atlantic Ocean, on the farthest corner of their lot, the Burruses initiated skating there. The same wood floor functioned for both skating and dancing at different times. Perhaps skating was a weeknight activity while the floor was reserved for weekend dancing.

When we were still too young to go alone, Connie Ballance's parents, Cecil and Mary Ballance, younger than mine, sometimes took us to the dance hall to watch. Connie and I attempted our first dance steps together. If we were fortunate enough, some young fellow would ask us to dance. It may have been on a lark for them, but to two budding coquettes, it amounted to far more.

We loved square dancing. At Hatteras we made one large circle instead of several groups of four. The caller would instruct the dancers, while local musicians, like Theodore O'Neal on the fiddle and Lonie Stowe Styron (Austin) at the piano, provided the music. Many times these were impromptu dances.

Another dance hall owned by Harry Austin did not last long. Located nearer the ocean, it washed down in a storm and was never replaced.

Albert Lyons of Detroit, Michigan, gave the Hatteras Girls' Club, a generous gift, to Hatteras girls in the early 1930s. Our benefactor provided shuffleboards, Ping-Pong tables, and magazines. Perhaps his dream failed because leadership he sent left before local leadership could be trained. Many, particularly those who were teenagers then, remember the benefits of having a club of their own. Their motto was, "He can, who thinks he can."

Mary Francis Sutherland came the first year to teach dancing and direct the program. Violet Gaskill Austin, in an interview for the Cape Hatteras High School publication, *Sea Chest*, some years ago told correspondents Belle Stowe and Faye Ballance about a musical review in which she dressed as a toy soldier. The community was invited to such special programs. Otherwise, only members who had paid their fees and been duly initiated were allowed access to the Hatteras Girls' Club.

Myrtle Gray Burrus recalled a party given for her before her marriage, July 5, 1929, to Herman Burrus. Gooseville Gun Club members, maybe Mr. Lyons, had flown in ice cream and special food for the July 4th celebration.

Ruth, Alivia, Aulise, and Achsah Burrus; Mary Elizabeth Styron; Grace Daily; and my sister Marjorie Austin called themselves the Yoo-Hoo Gang. With other young women of the community from 18 to 28, they enjoyed their membership privileges at the Hatteras Girls' Club for several years. Even younger ones like me were introduced to tap dance by Miss Sutherland on Saturday mornings in that beautiful new building with polished oak floors, shiny mahogany furniture, and pretty, flowery, bright drapes. We had never seen such luxury before.

Another special feature was the cement tennis court, where Mr. Lyons and his friends could play when they were in the village. A few locals had already learned the game and enjoyed the court. Perhaps someone gave lessons. That big expanse of concrete has served much longer as a parking lot than it ever did as a tennis court. It is still in place for parking for the Hatteras Health Center and is used by Hatteras United Methodist Church.

After the Girls' Club folded, the building was sometimes used by special permission for community affairs. Had the community been ready for it then, it would have made a fine community building. Instead, it served the community in several very different ways.

As a medical center, the building was where Dr. Crankshaw, with the help of a local nurse, did surgery and delivered babies before World War II. At the height of the submarine threat off our coast during the war, it housed a Sub Station, from which crew members, on horseback, patrolled our beach as part of U. S. Coast Guard vigilance. For a number of years, it housed the United States Weather Bureau before headquarters were moved to Buxton. During that time, part of it was subdivided into apartments. The building was later torn down, and the site is now occupied by the present community medical center.

William T. (Scotty) Gibson came to Hatteras with the Works Project Administration project, married Nettie Robinson, and stayed. In 1937 he rented the property, including the Pavillion and Hotel, from Corlette and Rebecca (Beck) Burrus. In 1945, Scotty purchased it.

During WW II, Gibson reopened The Pavillion. Someone nicknamed it "The Bird Cage." A bird could fly in the front door and out the back door, but rabbit wire on the windows could keep them out or in when those doors were closed. However, the rabbit wire did not keep out the mosquitoes.

A jukebox provided music for dancing, i.e., "Racing With The Moon," "You Only Hurt The One You Love," and "Three Little Fishes." Beer was available at the counter, but most girls in our crowd neither drank nor smoked.

During my last year of high school, 1942-43, we sometimes gathered and danced in the building that now houses The Channel Bass Restaurant. It was originally built by Uncle Horton Austin, Brother Shanklin, and Donald Oden. Mr. Ogden baked bread, delicious pies, beautiful birthday cakes, and scrumptious cookies and pastries there. Linwood Ballance delivered bread all the way to Rodanthe, before pavement came. The enterprise was very successful.

Mr. Ogden roomed at our house. After several months, he left to go to Norfolk to shop and never returned. Daddy blamed himself, thinking his curiosity about his family had prompted him to escape. We never knew about his family or why he did not return.

After his abrupt departure, the owners were able to contact and employ a Mr. White to take his place. White had resided in Hatteras some years before and had a bakery in the shop between our home and the Methodist Parsonage in earlier years. However, he did not stay long. I am unsure why the thriving business failed. Mama supposed the addition of beer sales in the front part of the building accounted for its downfall.

In cold weather, we liked the bakery building. The front was a warmer, nicer place to gather, even though the dance area was small, and there were no benches like in the other places. We stood, leaning against the walls. Thinking about that, I thought perhaps the lingering cigarette smoke bothered both Ogden's and White's sense of purity and interfered with the aroma of fresh baking.

Sometime during the same period, we met and danced at Willard Burrus' Beacon, a plain rectangular building with a single light bulb above the front door, hence its name. Before and during the war years, we jammed the place on Friday and Saturday nights after the movie at Austin Theater.

Austin Theater, built and equipped with modern machinery in 1935- 36 by my father for brother Shank, employed Corlette Burrus as projectionist. Corlette taught my brother Shank. When Corlette sold the Atlantic View Hotel to Scotty Gibson and moved to Norfolk, Shank became the primary projectionist.

When Shank went into the U. S. Army, I became the manager and sold tickets for six movies a week. Shank had taught a couple of high school boys, who became our projectionists. First, Clyde Austin, and later, Buster (Lionel) Ballance took care of the projection room.

One night during that time we had a crisis. I sold tickets and was watching from the ticket booth when the screen suddenly turned red and someone yelled, "Fire!" In a panic, I ran out of the building with the idea of getting additional fire extinguishers from our house and Austin Store next door. However, they were never needed. Buster, younger than I, showed great presence of mind. Right by the projector, he ripped the burning celluloid film out of the projector and threw it where it could not hurt anything. A metal, looking like lead, completely covered the walls, floors, and ceiling of the room where the two projectors were housed. I do not think it could have been aluminum. Aluminum was not as widely used in 1943 as it is now. It may have been steel, but I think it was lead.

After splicing the two broken ends together, Buster finished showing the movie. But I was so shook up that I never got back to the theater and felt ashamed for what looked like cowardice and abandonment on my part. The responsibility for all those lives, the building, and everything seemed squarely on my seventeen-year-old shoulders, and I had failed. No one confronted me, and I could not even talk about it.

Three films, each shown twice, added up to the six movies a week. Shank scheduled special midnight movies on Christmas Eve and New Year's Eve. We probably continued that tradition while he was gone to the war. The responsibility for contracting with the film companies was mine. A certain number of B films had to be included with those considered A, which were the more popular films with the movie idols and queens of the silver screen. All of these came to us by mail in metal containers. As soon as they had been shown, they had to be sealed up and mailed back. When a film did not arrive on time for a showing, we had a crisis. That happened. Sometimes it arrived late and was shown anyway. At other times, Shank might have shown one not yet returned for the third showing in its place.

Movies brought people to Hatteras from the other six villages up the beach, even from Rodanthe about 40 miles away, and before the paved road. Servicemen came from the Coast Guard Stations—Cape Hatteras, Creeds Hill, and Hatteras Inlet. Sometimes fishermen from Ocracoke or Core Sound were part of the crowd at the movies and the dance hall any night of the week. Songs of the forties—"Chattanooga Choo Choo," "The Jersey Bounce," "Don't Get Around Much Anymore," "White Cliffs of Dover," "Beer Barrel Polka," "When The Lights Go On Again All Over The World"—gave musical background. Jitterbugging was the craze. Some servicemen, particularly from New Jersey, helped us appreciate the polka and taught us how.

In the summer we sweltered, fought mosquitoes; in the winter we danced faster to keep warm. Neither the Beacon nor the Bird Cage had heat or screens. Air conditioning was a long way in the future.

It was during the war years. With submarines sinking ships off the shore, the windows had to have dark shades, and the upper part of car lights were painted black so the rays would not attract the submarines off our shore. We could see the fires of the ships burning offshore. Shank, while driving the beach to the Oregon Inlet ferry to bring home for leave some of the local men who were part of the merchant marines and vital to the United States during World War II, found a body on the shore one morning. The body came from one of the ships or submarines destroyed off shore.

There are still boats, boats with high-powered motors. There are still beach parties, crab feasts, and private parties. Maybe some visit at the stores. There may still be wild grapes on The Hills. But no theater exists at Hatteras, nor is there a place for young folks to dance. Ice cream is easy to obtain. However, there are no longer easy, available gathering places for people to dance, to visit, and to enjoy one another and share their lives. The Hatteras Civic Center is available for parties. The Hatteras Community Center is used for all kinds of community functions and social gatherings. A bridge over Oregon Inlet, ferries that run day and night across Hatteras Inlet, television, videocassette recorders, and computers have changed our lives forever. This is the electronic age, and the character of Hatteras has changed as much as its landscape, with large, expensive homes and excessive traffic.

A portion of this piece has appeared in *The Island Breeze*.

Sybil after a tap dancing lesson in front of the Hatteras Girl's Club

"Little Darlings" Sybil and Mona

Front row, L. to R.: Leola Austin, Velma Austin, Minerva Austin, Elsie Ballance, Careda Willis, Hazel Gaskill. Back row, L. to R.: Marian Burrus, Anna Ballance, Marcella Burrus, Sybil

The seventh grade class of Hatteras School. Back Row, L. to R.: Teacher Hilda Ballance Brown, Marcella Barrus, Velma Morris, Daisy Stowe, Sybil; Middle row: "Barney" Austin, Freeman Meekins, Leola Austin, Velma Austin, Elsie Ballance, Martha Gaskins, Anna Ballance, Hydous Austin, Army O'Neal, Keith Peele. Front Row: "Bud" West, Freeman Stowe, David Austin, Clyde Austin, Edgar "Corky" Burrus, Gaston Foster, Sherrill Gibbs.

Daddy and Mama

The family after a crab feast at Hatteras in 1942: Brother Shank is home on leave from the army. Josephine, Curtis Newton, Margie, Shank's wife, Ruby, Sybil with Mona behind her

Eula Williams' piano students. Sybil is in the back row, second from right

Hal Gray with Marian Burrus, the "frog-spotter"

Good friends (L. to R.): Ruby Aust Marcella Burrus, Connie Ballance, Louise Oden, Lucy Stowe

Sybil at her high school graduation in 1943 with Elsie Ballance,
left, and the school's mascot, Joey
Fagley. Sybil's house is in the
background.

Three inspiring teachers, Margaret
Morris, English; Elizabeth Baum,
History; Alton Baum, Math. Sheila
Gibson, the school's 1942 mascot,
is in front.

Sybil got her middle name from "Doc" Maurice Bernard Folb, who delivered her

Mona with Clyde Talent, a science teacher. Sybil's piano playing sent him from the room.

Sybil while a student at UNC, 1945

Don Skakle at UNC, 1945

Sybil and Don at their marriage ceremony in Chapel Hill, NC, with Rev. Charles Jones and witnesses Frank and Betty Zimmerman

Chapter 15
Pretense and Performance

❦

eems to me, we had many chances to be inventive and imaginative when we were growing up at Hatteras. Before movies or television, we entertained ourselves by acting out our interpretations of the songs we heard and knew from the radio or the old Victrola records. Before I could read the labels, I used to wind the old Victrola with a handle and try to choose, sometimes by the color of the records themselves, the one I wanted to hear. I liked, "Hand Me Down My Walking Cane. Hand me down my walking cane, Hand me down my walking cane, I'm going to leave on the midnight train...". There was another orange one that I did not like nearly as well.

We little girls loved to sing and perform "Frankie and Johnnie" on our front porch or out in our side yard. While there were other songs, that one gave us certain opportunities. Having pledged undying love to one another, when Johnnie finds Frankie "loving up that high brow Nellie Bly," she shoots him dead. The police come, arrest Johnnie, put her in jail and "throw the key away." And the funeral party! "Seven men going to the graveyard, only six men coming back!" These scenes provided wonderful material for us to be dramatic and morbid. Think of those plodding pallbearers and the wailing mourners!

Such high moments of drama persuaded one of our numbers,

Connie Ballance, to engage her family's outside shed, or "crib," for what we expected to be the finest production ever. There would even be an admission charge. Several of us—Marian Burrus, Louise Oden, Marcella Burrus—lived close to the home of Connie's parents, Cecil and Mary Ballance. We spent a considerable time planning our program and preparing our performance area.

Sad to say, that dream of riches did not materialize and was no more successful than some of our other business ventures—a gypsy tearoom, outside, where we served yaupon tea; a store under the front, outside steps where our customers had to crawl on hands and knees to get under the steps. A very large packing box that had come to Daddy's store holding bolts of cloth inspired another store. My friend Marian Burrus and I became engaged in the frog business. She was afraid one would pee on her and give her warts, so she acted as spotter and I picked them up to deposit them into the round, empty cheese box from Daddy's store.

We never made a single sale from our cheese box, nor sold a single ticket for our show. Our attempt at a beauty shop in a room of the old school house found us washing hair in an enamel wash pan. Clyde Austin paid us to do his hair, and Mama submitted to a manicure until I made her cuticle bleed by cutting it too close. We definitely needed training and equipment!

Even though our variety show and other ventures failed, they kept a bunch of little girls happily engaged for many hours in creative play. Other than our homemade entertainment, there were grade school operettas at the end of the school year. Our mothers made crepe paper costumes to dress us up like angels, fairies, or flowers, all very colorful!

At a first grade dress rehearsal, I tore my white, fairy wing on the potbelly stove door handle as we waited to go on stage. My first grade teacher, Miss Robinson, distraught and nervous, overreacted and slapped my face. I did not understand. After all, it was Mama who had to redo that wing before our performance that night.

I forgave Miss Robinson. Children learn early that being careful is not always enough, especially when you have unaccustomed wings attached to your shoulders. Children must learn to be patient and wise to keep from getting into trouble with irritable, responsible adults, who do not always see the truth of what is happening with children. Children start early to grow wise.

Oxford Baptist Orphanage brought a group fairly regularly, it seemed. Local people provided room and board for them, and we children enjoyed having new, young blood in our midst. A love offering to help defray their traveling expenses may have been the financial arrangement. They could not have received much. But their performance provided diversion for them and for us.

Other professional or semiprofessional groups came. Who engaged them or why they were chosen is a question. There was an admission charge. That meant it benefited some organization in the community.

Once, a girl my age and her father showed up to ask my brother Shanklin to give her a chance to perform on the stage of Austin Movie Theater. About 1938, like so many others, they sought every means possible to live during the worst financial crisis ever known, called The Great Depression. She gave a performance in front of the silver screen prior to a movie one night, singing and dancing. She was not a professional, but we were hungry for entertainment. Maybe they collected a few nickels and dimes.

Robinson's Medicine Show came one summer. For several nights, Mr. Robinson hawked his patent medicine and sold bags of taffy with cheap prizes inside. There were several blacks. My favorite, Snookums, could tap dance and sing! They were housed in an unpainted shop my father owned, next to our yard. When Snookums practiced beyond our fence, "Climb Upon My Knee, Sonny Boy," our dog stood by the white fence palings and howled to accompany him.

I hated to see that group leave. Every night I had been near their tent in the Hatteras School yard, across from our home, looking for a prize in a bag of taffy.

Sometimes the women got together their own shows. I particularly remember a womanless wedding. The groom, Mr. Richard Dailey, Hatteras Weather Bureau director and the handsome husband of Dinah O'Neal, had as his bride short, stocky Mr. Gibson, one of the high school teachers. They looked funny together. All were delighted, except for the little boy who put a penny in one of the footlight sockets that did not have a bulb. He received a shock and a very sore finger.

My Mama was a wedding guest and rode me around in a baby carriage. Eight, nine, or ten, with my legs dangling over the side, I pretended to cry. Mama stuck a raw hot dog in my mouth. She had a bottle of milk available for me to wash it down. Wieners still taste good to me.

Mr. Alton Baum, the principal of the Hatteras High School for several years, had us practice for end-of-school festivities. Under his direction, I learned to sing a part other than the melody in some of the classical choruses. I felt good about that. How grateful I am for his presence in my life! He taught math also. His wife Elizabeth was one of the best history teachers I ever knew, even in college. Mr. Baum was a very fine math teacher. I believe I still remember how to solve a square root.

Mr. Baum undertook to teach us social manners. Years later, my children had Mrs. Helen Bagby in Chapel Hill. In Hatteras, it was Mr. Baum who coached the boys to seat their dates and use the right eating utensil at the banquet, and the girls how to fill out their dance cards.

Elizabeth and Alton married late and had no children while they were with us. They gave us all they could while they remained with us. After they left Hatteras and went to Washington, North Carolina, they had a son Walter—now a jeweler in Chapel Hill—and a daughter Nancy.

Every year the school gave plays, directed by the current English teacher. What fun! My junior year I had a character part, an older, unmarried woman, who cried a lot. As that character, I became someone different from myself. I enjoyed that role much more than the romantic one in my senior year, in which Levin Stowe played my fiancé.

However, the most memorable of all shows at Hatteras for me was "The Rehearsal of a Gay Nineties Review." Done sometime during the four years between 1954 and 1958, probably 1956, when Don, our sons, and I were living at Hatteras, it stands out as a bright jewel of experience.

Don overtaxed his energies and emotions—it's now called "burn out"—teaching junior high school, coaching the senior high tennis team in the Greensboro schools, and acting as tennis professional during the summers at the Greensboro Country Club. At Hatteras, with a complete change of interest and pace, Don recovered in about six months, but we stayed on for four years. Our youngest son was born at the Cape Hatteras Health Center in October 1956.

We lived with my parents. Don managed and clerked at Austin's Store. I kept the house and took care of the apartments in the house, while Mama taught school. Daddy hoped we would be content to stay and make Hatteras our home. But that's another story.

Locals got together to put on a show. It was initiated by Lillie Oden Peele to benefit the Hatteras Library, housed in the old Hatteras School building, which functioned as a community building until it was demolished. (A new community building, built on the same site, houses the new Hatteras Library, a source of pride and enjoyment to the community.)

Delores Burrus and Virginia Hudgins were members of the library committee and were asked to bring some type of entertainment suggestion to the meetings. Someone had the idea that a show of some sort would be the thing, with proceeds earmarked for the library. Delores was asked to write a show. She did, directed it, and took part in the delightful variety show, which she called "A Rehearsal of a Gay Nineties Review." "In case it be a flop," she quips, "I could then say, 'Well, it was only a rehearsal!' "

The admission charge was right, a quarter for a child and fifty cents for an adult. We played to a full house, with many standing, for three Saturday nights in succession. Some tourists came to see the show. Don, excited by our efforts, did a lot of by-mouth advertising as he did business.

Presented as a practice, the show changed every night, according to the imagination of someone in the group. "Where Did You Get That Hat" brought three guys dressed like women on stage to sing. One night Don came on stage with a lampshade as his "tile."

We made our own nineteenth century costumes for the show. Some older members had clothing they could pull out of storage. Ones like Kate Harrell Austin Burrus and Lovie O'Neal Burrus had been part of the era, when their dress preceded the short skirts of the flappers and the Charleston of the Roaring Twenties.

Alice Gray gave of her time and talent to play the piano. Margaret Willis Peele sang "Shine On Harvest Moon." Don and I did "Daisy." In addition to the original verse, we wrote one for me to sing to him. Gamaliel and Wheeler Ballance, Frank Gaskins, and a fourth person—Fulton Scarborough or maybe Don—made up the barber shop quartet. They wore striped shirts with garters holding up their sleeves, flat straw show hats, spats on their shoes, and sported handlebar mustaches.

The setting of the said rehearsal was in the garden of a fairly well-to-do couple. Lona Styron played their maid Roxanne and Jimmy Cox their gardener, whose stage name was Bill Bailey. Lona and Jimmy Cox—in black face—did a cute skit featuring, "Won't You Come Home, Bill Bailey?"

Delores sang "Alice Blue Gown" and made the black bathing suits Lizzie Austin and Robert Hudgins wore when they sang "By the Sea, By the Sea, By the Wonderful Sea." She remembers that a romance between Cox and Jeanne Gray grew out of that show. Their marriage endured until Jimmy's death. Our practices were highlights of those weeks prior to its presentation.

Charlotte Ballance, our most avid supporter, Delores recalls, never missed a performance. She claimed her seat, early, each night.

The stage was decorated with lovely, local flowers in bloom from our yards, and we lit up all the footlights on the old auditorium stage and added more. All the members of the cast offered their talents and service. The ladies made their dresses with bustles and found old hats and decorated them.

The show closed with "May the Good Lord Bless and Keep You." Happy and satisfied, we took our bows. With entertainment prevalent and television readily available, it is easy to forget the fun it is to be part of a performance.

These days, I belong to a group called the Chapel Hill Village Revue. All volunteers, we do vaudeville type shows for seniors at the retirement homes and rehabilitation and nursing homes. As a payback, for the use of the auditorium for our two-hour practice each Tuesday, we do shows for regulars at the Chapel Hill Senior Center. We are seniors entertaining seniors, when we sing from our hearts and to encourage ourselves and others, "I'm Going To Live 'til I Die," or "The Best of Times Are Now." It helps us believe that life can still be good, whatever our circumstances. Making others smile lifts our own spirits. "There's no business like show business."

Chapter 16
Mystery of Male

My only brother, ten years older, like my father seemed from another planet. We ate meals together, but they were a mystery, surrounded as I was by sisters and Mama, with whom I did girl things—cooking, cleaning, washing. etc. By observation, I knew what men did. Daddy, next door in the store, was available and observable to us most of the time. Later, I learned that males have similar feelings, but they do think differently.

Once, when we were little, Daddy let Mona and me go down to Austin Creek with him. He was building a boat, a trim little craft he named Ramona. In our bathing suits, Mona and I played all day at the water's edge, keeping ourselves amused, stuffing our bathing suits with jellyfish until we were tired and hungry. Daddy, in the middle of a task, put us off until we were very tired and very hungry. I suppose we were not as anxious to go with him another time.

Also, I remember being with him at some time when he built the "Sybil" in the Gooseville Gun Club plane hangar, The United States Government bought the "Sybil", a fishing boat, from Daddy during the second World War. I saw it docked near the Berkley-Norfolk Ferry one summer before I knew that he had sold it to the government. I watched him build a third boat in the yard behind the store and house. However, I never drove a nail in one of the boats.

Well, male mystery translated into early curiosity for me about little boys. Even before the first grade, a pretty little boy with dark, wavy hair, the nephew of Beck Burrus, a dear friend of Mama's and mine, entranced me. I loved to spend time with Beck Burrus. I would walk out to the hotel where she and her husband Corlette lived—not always asking if I could go. To make my trip shorter, I walked on tussocks over a marshy place beyond the Slash Bridge and Willie Willis' home to get there. Oh, to be as nimble footed as I was then! Beyond the marsh, the road resumed again in front of Dick Austin's and continued to snake around until it reached the Atlantic View Hotel.

Rebecca Gaskins Burrus had beautiful, flawless skin, lovely brown eyes and always smelled of Coty L'Origan face powder. I adored her, and she seemed to appreciate my attention before the birth of her son Winston.

One night after the picture show at The Pavilion, in front of the hotel where Beck had an apartment, I stopped by to see her. Her nephew was visiting. Junnie Jeanette was such a pretty little boy that I wanted to stay with her and watch him. When I learned he and his mother were staying overnight with Beck and Corlette. I decided I should stay, too. Alas, Mama and Daddy came for me, and I went home reluctantly. It may have been rivalry more than attraction for the little boy, but I do not think so. I liked that little boy.

The next male encounter that I remember concerned books. We bought our books for school each year. My reader that year was brand new and created an obstacle for me because it was whole. When a page was gone, as they might be from a second-hand book, we were permitted to sit with someone else to read. I wanted that privilege. So in second grade, I committed the unforgivable by tearing my new book so I could sit with a little blond boy I liked. That did not turn out well. He had a bed-wetting problem and had not bathed that morning. That cured me of defacing books forever. Even now, I mark books reluctantly and do not tear or dog-ear pages ever. Nor do I break their backs by turning them on their faces. Books are to be treated as cherished friends, lovingly and carefully.

Someone has said that play is children's work. We worked a lot. We jumped rope and played marbles. I had a favorite leader and challenged my cousin, David, and lost several marbles before I went home one afternoon.

Hop Scotch provided challenges. We drew three kinds in the dirt of the schoolyard and competed fiercely. One looked like a double winged airplane, another like a concentric circle, and the other was a square with three or four spaces on each side. We had our lucky shells for throwing. I identified my last little blue purse on the Norfolk trolley when visiting Aunt Rado one summer by saying to the conductor, "It has my lucky shell in it." He chuckled and handed me my lost pocketbook.

We had no regular sporting equipment. I expect we were no poorer than many other rural areas of North Carolina in the thirties. If someone had a ball, a game of cat would be initiated. A fence paling or a stick of some kind served as our bat.

Cat, the one ball game I had ever played, did not prepare me for baseball. As older youth, a crowd of us picked up a game at the ball diamond out on the road near the hotel and beach one summer afternoon. I threw a baseball and hit a friend in the back. Was he surprised! Our "cat," like tag ball, used a soft rubber ball.

Bob jacks kept us busy for hours. It took much skill to go through the whole game, until one scooped up all the jacks in one bounce of the small rubber ball. With the jacks, that tiny rubber ball, an opponent, and a flat, hard surface, we could begin the game and be engaged for hours. Girls played jacks more than the boys.

Mama taught us to make Tom Walkers from cans. We made two holes in the uncut end of like cans and threaded ropes through them. We slipped our feet into the space on top of the can and held the ropes tight to walk on them. They cut the ground beneath them.

Rolling hoops took skill and practice. One hoop appeared, and everyone felt they had to have one also. They were fun.

When Mr. Baum was our principal, he planned a field day. Students competed in foot races and jumping contests. It seems a discus appeared from somewhere. Maybe he acquired a javelin, too.

Of course, you understand that all the work-play we did was more fun if boys were part of it. We made paper money and after school ran through the rushes and weeds of Mr. Charlie Styron's lot playing cops and robbers. The money was for ransom payments.

But it bothered me when I was about twelve that Mama made a comment about how when little boys and girls get a certain age, they begin "to smell around." Did it remind me of the torn book incident? Did I think about dogs? The new feelings, uncomfortable and exciting, were embarrassing enough. Self-conscious enough, I did not like Mama to notice, but it changed nothing. I liked the boys, and they liked me. Two even had a fistfight over me.

Our Sunday afternoon walks to the beach in mixed crowds became part of our passage. Sunday school in the morning, our lunches, and then by plan or design boys and girls gathered to walk down to the seashore. One day one of the little boys had these white balloons that he filled up with ocean water. Those particular "balloons" expanded to a great degree. As I was wondering about them, a cousin of mine told me, "It's not a balloon, Sybil. It's a rubber!" She explained to me a very interesting activity among our parents.

One Sunday afternoon, several little girls and I volunteered to teach male friends to kiss. We chose Mr. Reuben Ballance's garage as the site of their education. I wonder if their future sweethearts and wives appreciated our efforts to teach them that a kiss needs to be gentle and lingering, with lips slightly parted and yielding. An open mouth is threatening. No one wants to be slobbered on or swallowed. A kiss should be moist, but not wet. Did I know that at ten?

Somewhere along the way, I read that it is desirable for young people to date many different persons, like twenty-five, before choosing one for a lifetime mate. "Window shop a long time before choosing." I did my best.

Our "dates" were having a fellow walk us home from the Beacon, where we assembled to dance and observe. Boys from Frisco, Buxton, and Avon "dated" Hatteras girls, and Hatteras swains sought to form liaisons with girls from those other villages. Of course, there was a great deal of rivalry between the boys of the several villages, but for the most part they were friendly to one another.

Our early date scenario included a trek through mosquitoes in summer time or cold in winter, holding hands, as we walked home in the sand ruts, a goodnight kiss, and good-bye! That was it. Truly, there is "safety in numbers" for boy and girl gatherings. While we had not analyzed that saying, we practiced it as early adolescents. Even walking home, we were in groups. Dating different persons and dating in groups kept individuals from getting too serious, too soon. We were too young for permanent commitments. We were enjoying the game of collecting "scalps," so to speak. Every gathering carried questions, "How many boys will ask to walk me home?" "Will I choose too soon and be stuck with someone when I want to be with someone who asks me after all? "

Cut off as we were from the mainland, families knew one another. Our parents, in my case my father, had grown up with the fathers and mothers of the boys who walked me home. Therefore, I think we had the same rules and expectations. Even when the servicemen came later, as a consequence of World War II and the need for greater surveillance of the coast against submarine invasion, the men in charge of the several stations were usually local men. Perhaps they explained the rules and regulations of acceptable social encounters to the young men under them. Young like we ourselves, perhaps their families and communities had similar values, although they came from North, South, and Midwest.

For a short time, I dated a Coast Guard man from Philadelphia. A wonderful dancer, he had a red convertible, and I was in heaven until I learned that he had a wife back home. One of the guys from his station told my sister that he had gone home and discussed divorce with his wife. Dismayed, not wanting to ever hurt another woman, I did not continue seeing him. I grieved and cried a lot. My regrets were minor. Our relationship had been platonic. When he later brought his lovely young wife to Hatteras Island, I met and liked her. I hope they made it through the war and life together.

About the time this happened to me, a boy from Buxton, who had finished school in Wilmington, Delaware, living with an older sister, came home to Buxton. He intended to enlist in the Coast Guard before he would be drafted. His father was an officer at the Cape Hatteras Coast Guard Station, and, like many other boys, he would follow his father and older brothers into that branch of the service. He had already lost a brother, the first casualty of World War II from Dare County. When I learned Thomas Midgett had been killed, I sat at my school desk and composed a letter of condolence. Our correspondence continued until he came home.

George had walked me home a few times before he went to Delaware. He had seemed so intense that I told him, "I like you, but I don't want to date you." He was standing in the doorway of the Beacon, while I stood on the ground looking up at him.

However, the script played out this way. George came home, sympathetic and attentive. Chafing under the injury to my pride and my disappointment—maybe on the rebound—I appreciated having George there to date. We became a pair in the crowd.

George did not own a vehicle. He relied on rides with those who did come to Hatteras, ten miles from Buxton, to see me. One night he got left and walked all the way home, arriving sometime early next morning. Mama said, "It must be love."

When I was seventeen in January, in my last year in high school, distractions were part of my life. Shank had been called into the Army, leaving me to manage Austin Theater. Besides that, I worked in the store and helped in the house. I finished first in my class of nine, not sure I really deserved it. School was not memorable. Mr.

Hipp, our principal, seemed distracted himself. Some said that when he sometimes left school in the middle of a class, it was to go down to get a beer at the place across the Slash Bridge.

After George joined the Coast Guard, he went to Manhatten Beach for boot camp. We wrote frequently. We had an understanding. When it came time for my senior prom, with his knowledge, I invited Tony, an Italian from Brooklyn, New York, in the Coast Guard at Hatteras. He was another's sweetheart. He married a local girl, Martha Gaskins. She may be able to spell his last name. I do not dare try.

That summer after graduation, Mama went with me to McPherson Eye, Ear, Nose, and Throat Hospital for an operation to align my left eye. I had worn glasses since I was five years old when it had been discovered at Daddy's store, probably by a visiting optician, that I had a lazy eye. Daddy's store, centrally located, had a space that could be used by such professionals. The room, called the phone room, where three rings signaled someone at Austin Store to pick up the phone, provided that space.

Dr. Woodard, in that same room, set up his dental equipment to take care of Hatteras children. Perhaps the county sent him for those irregular visits. His slow drill was powered, much like the old sewing machines, by a foot pedal, and it was a torture machine. I chose to have teeth pulled instead of filled.

I remember terrible toothaches, of lying on my back in the floor and kicking my feet in the air to relieve the pain. I remember crawling into bed with Mama and Daddy and having Mama hold an aspirin on an aching tooth, cradling my cheek on her soft, warm arm until it stopped hurting, and I could drop off to sleep.

But the eye doctor decided I had a "lazy eye," which develops in childhood when the information traveling from two eyes to the brain is different, and two images cannot be overlapped easily. The brain, confused, suppresses the eye responsible for the conflicting information, and the visual acuity of that eye drops. Treatment is best done before eight years of age. Advised to wear a patch on the right eye, an attempt to strengthen the vision in the left, I failed. Mama could not be with me all the time. I could not be bothered. A Norfolk eye surgeon, to whom my parents took me, advised full maturity before an operation.

So, at seventeen, I anticipated having the eye operated on and having my nice brown eyes beautifully aligned at last. I had been self-conscious about my eye. Kids are sometimes cruel. Now you understand why my eye operation is part of the mystery between girls and boys. I wanted to be attractive to the young men in my life.

When I went in for eye surgery the summer of 1943, a three-year-old girl was having the operation. Her results were probably better than mine. In the intervening years, ideas had changed, or the Norfolk doctor had been ignorant of the advances. Now the surgery is done early to align the eye so the eye will not become lazy.

For three days both my eyes were covered. It was summer and hot. The adhesive that held the bandage over my eyes was miserable. Blinded, nevertheless I wrote my usual letter to George. Mama came back from lunch one day to find I had scrawled all over an unfinished letter of hers.

When bandages were removed, I looked into the mirror to see a terrible looking eye. My iris seemed lost in the red, muddy eye mass. While we waited for my stitches to be removed, Mama had a nose operation to straighten a crooked septum. Today, they would have sent me out of there in a day or two.

After we were released, we took a bus and traveled to Bainbridge, Maryland, to visit my sister Jo, who had married her childhood sweetheart, Carlos Oden, from Hatteras. He was a naval chief. Jo had a clerical job.

Bainbridge, a training base, maintained high security during wartime. When I went to the commissary within the compound, a fellow behind the meat counter asked me to go out with him. I accepted. He picked me up at the apartment, and we drove to Havre de Grace to an eating place and visited awhile over a bowl of ice cream. We drove back and could not find the right gate to get us back into the Bainbridge compound. I began to have misgivings about going out with this strange fellow. I tried not to show my anxiety. I could see he was upset enough. Finally, we found "a" gate and he said to the two guards, "Please, let us pass. I really need to get this girl back to her family."

Thankfully, they let us through. When we got back to the apartment, Mama was coming down the walk with a kerchief on her head. "Mama, where are you going?" I asked.

"To look for you!" she said.

"Mama," I said, my stomach still knotted with anxiety, "you would never have found us." I told her that we had been riding around outside the base for over an hour—maybe two—trying to find the right gate.

Poor Mama! Bainbridge, Maryland, was very different from Hatteras, North Carolina. At home she came to look for us if we were late coming home. You can believe that was not often. Mama's protectiveness acted as an effective incentive to be home before expected. Knowing her reaction pattern had added to my disquiet that evening. I never wanted to displease either of my parents. My need for their favor and approval kept me straight through the tempestuous emotions of teenage years. Their rules were a chain fence that kept me from plunging over the cliff into sexual gratification. Alcohol did not tempt me, and Mama had discouraged me from cigarettes at ten when she found me behind the chimney in the room where Mona and I slept, smoking one of hers. That was the day we both stopped smoking forever.

My parents' trust, the strong moral code of my community, my faith in God, the fear of pregnancy, and the desire to wait for the man I would eventually marry were powerful deterrents. Was I tempted? Of course, I was! However, those I dated had fears and had respect for my parents and me as we had for their parents and them.

Jo and Carlos had given me permission to invite George to come from Manhattan Beach to their place for the weekend. George and I had talked of marriage, but were not officially engaged at that time.

We went to a USO show Sunday afternoon in Bainbridge. When we walked into the stands, a cry went up from all those fellows in naval uniforms: "What is that Coast Guardsman doing here with that girl?"

Well-known movie star Joan Blondell was one of the performers. I knew then, but not now, who the other performers were. She sang, "I'm in the Mood for Love." She quipped about the line, "If it should rain, we'll let it? / And who thinks they can keep it from raining?"

Mama and I left by train, and George left to go back to his camp. We cried when we said good-bye. Our train was crowded, like other public conveyances during the war. Cinders came in through the windows. I had to sit on my suitcase part of the way. We got to Norfolk early the next morning and stopped off for a visit with Aunt Rado in Berkley before going home to Hatteras. The discoloration in and around the operated eye had improved. I resumed my responsibilities, clerking in the store and managing the theater since Shank was drafted into the Army.

Soon after we came home, an engagement ring arrived in the mail for me from George, and I began to plan for a wedding in December during his leave. Mama said, " When two fools make up their minds, you might as well go along with them."

I had planned to follow my older siblings and go to college. But George said, "If you love me, you'll marry me instead of going to college." My romantic heart agreed. I stayed home to work in the store and theater, waiting to marry him. I visited his family in Buxton, planning for a wedding and Christmas, crocheting treasurers for my "hope chest."

Blood tests, required then, had to be acquired by mail. Licenses, too. His father, Mr. Willie Midgett, came to Hatteras and took me to the Coast Guard infirmary up at Cape Hatteras Station in Buxton to have my blood drawn to mail away.

I wrote George daily, finding poems to express my feelings: "The only thing that matters is that you are there / And I am here without you. /

And it's lonely everywhere." The songs of the forties echoed the emotions of my heart: "Don't Get Around Much Anymore," "I'll Walk Alone," "I Just Kissed Your Picture Goodnight."

My friend Marian, living with her sister and brother-in-law, Grace and Henry Bland, in Florida, had a very responsible job folding parachutes to help the war effort. She agreed to be my maid of honor and quit her job to come home for Christmas and our wedding. She did not go back even after George's letter, which reminded me of that time when I had said I did not want to date him. He had met someone else. The wedding was cancelled.

His father, very distraught, said, "Don't give back the ring."

Connie's father Cecil said, "His head is like a door knob. Any girl can turn it."

Daddy said, "I wouldn't have said a thing, but I am glad you are not going to marry that boy."

Strange that I did not ask Daddy what he meant. I did not know how to reply. I said nothing.

Mama said: "The boys will be afraid of you for awhile."

That bothered me. I did not ask Mama what she meant, either. I thought I knew. It hurt to think that anyone would question my virtue.

Mama was wrong. I had always been popular with both the boys and the girls. Marian was home and Mace Quidley from Buxton, in the Coast Guard and stationed at Creeds Hill, were there for me. The three of us went around together. He got kidded about being chaperoned. Good natured, he laughed that away, and we continued our threesome.

Mama gave a dinner for me for my eighteenth birthday. Marian and Mace were among the friends invited. From the perspective of years, I know Mama intended to comfort and support me during a very difficult time. The truth was, I had no experience to prepare me for what had happened to me. I had been rejected. Defiant, I denied my feelings. My pride had been injured, I told myself. That's all. I had not really loved George. I'll show him! I thought.

He came home that summer, walked me home from the Beacon one night, and asked to see me the following Saturday night. I agreed but laid down an ultimatum, "If you do not keep the date, I'll never have anything more to do with you."

He went to Norfolk with his mother and did not get back. His mother told me years later, "It was my fault. I told him you would forgive him."

She was wrong. I did not forgive him. Instead, I cut him dead. Therefore, in my secret heart I believed that I could have had him back if I had not been too stubborn to forgive him. Since I had not given him a chance to explain, I felt that I shared the blame and guilt. We never talked; never had closure.

"You Always Hurt the One You Love," popular then, reminds me of sweet, smooth dancing, full-bodied Marty. He died in Japan, not from a war injury but of a supposed heart attack. A cousin, Gamaliel Ballance, on the same Coast Guard cutter gave me the news.

Marty Dudek, Coast Guardsman at the Hatteras Substation came from Passaic, New Jersey. I dated him a few times, He said, "You can't love me because you have been hurt."

He may have been right. I knew nothing about psychology then. I did not talk about my feelings. I did the best I knew how with my emotions and thoughts and internalized all my hurt, never fully aware of bitterness or vengeful feelings. Only now do I know how much that event affected my feelings about myself and how that deep wounding influenced my future relationships.

That summer, I dated Harold Webb, a member of the Hatteras Weather Bureau staff, proving to myself and to George, whom I had no contact with, that others found me attractive and good company. That fall, I left Hatteras Island to begin my college career. Hal Webb stopped by Greensboro to see me on his way back to his home in Mississippi. There he found someone to love and to love him. I had not yet met the person I loved more than my stubborn pride.

Chapter 17
Leaving Home

ccepted at the University of North Carolina for the first quar-ter, October 1944, I decided I wanted to go in September. Mama had a saying that applies to this situation. "It is easi-er to please a fool than to plague one." In pleasing me, she never tried to talk me out of that foolish notion. Instead, she found out when the semester began at Woman's College of UNC and deter-mined, since it began in September, I would go there. Mama fell off the ladder going into the attic the morning we were scheduled to go. Daddy, who did not think they could afford to send me to college, said, "Inez, maybe that means you should not go."

"The others have had their chance, and Sybil is going to have hers," she replied. So Mama and I were on the boat Hadeco when it sailed out of Rollinson Creek to go to Swan Quarter that day, and rode the bus all day long to arrive in Greensboro.

Jo and Carlos had moved home, and she had taken over my respon-sibilities for Austin Theater and Austin Store. Shank was in the U. S. Army Signal Corps, stationed somewhere in India, and showed movies to other soldiers.

Arriving in Greensboro, we went to the registrar's office at the col-lege without my having been accepted. All the freshman dorms were filled, but Mama managed to "matriculate" me. What a strange word! So my education began.

I was placed in a sophomore dorm, but I was told that I must observe freshman rules, which were quite restrictive and protective. We had to have permission slips signed by the housemother on duty to go off campus even with our own classmates and to have a date. Sometimes that entailed running all over campus to find the house-mother on duty. Rightfully, the administration needed to know where we might be found and who our companions were.

The girl whose room I took had to drop out of school due to her health. Her former roommate, Grace Brewer, a petite girl from eastern North Carolina, became mine. My first and lasting impression of our first meeting left me bewildered. I felt she resented rooming with a freshman and having me replace the other girl as her roommate. I never was able to get beyond that barrier. We never became true friends. She had friends from the year before among the sophomores. I made friends with other sophomore girls within the dorm, with those I ate with in the dining hall, and other classmates. There was one other girl from Buxton, Carol Miller, whom I already knew. She had planned to come all along and lived in a freshman dorm.

My plan from the beginning was to transfer to Carolina the following year. Jo had graduated in journalism from Carolina and told me that the only way a girl could go to Carolina before her junior year was as a nursing student or in something that sounded like "forestry." With so few trees at Hatteras, I did wonder about that. I cannot remember just how I learned the truth.

From September until Christmas was a very long time. When school broke for the holiday, I made that long bus trip, which took the whole day, to Swan Quarter. The boat was not waiting for me. I had to stay overnight in a rooming house, unsure and afraid.

Next day, on the boat crossing Pamlico Sound, I worried about my sister Mona. Mama had told me that one side of her beautiful face had frozen with something doctors called Bell's Palsy. Thank goodness, all the paralysis went away, but lying in the bunk of the Hadeco going home, I did not know that it would and could think of nothing else. My dread and helplessness made me miserable and afraid. We never knew the cause.

When I finally got home, I told Mama that I did not want to go back to school. Having known so much responsibility at home and having only the care of myself at school made me feel pampered and useless. Mama did not argue. Perhaps she knew that I would change my mind after two weeks. I did. Home had not measured up to my homesick fantasies—not a single red carpet! I was ready to return to biology, chemistry, Latin, English, math, and Greek mythology and my new friends.

Jo thought I would not like Woman's College with all the girls. She labeled me "boy crazy." Maybe I thought I would take a stab at it to prove or disprove her statement. There were a lot of girls! However, I learned good study habits and found very good teachers and some bright spots in the experience.

After Christmas, I even met a lovely young soldier, stationed at Bessemer ORD, waiting to be shipped overseas. Other girls and I attended a youth group at a Presbyterian Church near the campus. We did a skit and I had conversation with Calvin Bourgeault from Conshohocken, Pennsylvania, and his friends. The fellows walked us home after the youth group, and I asked Cal if he would like to attend the Sigmund Romberg Concert on campus. Romberg, a Hungarian-American composer, who lived between 1887-1951, wrote over seventy romantic operettas, including The Student Prince (1924), The Desert Song (1926), and The New Moon (1928). I loved his songs, especially "Smoke Gets in Your Eyes" from Roberta. Obviously on tour, he had his entourage in Greensboro my freshman year, and we heard him in the auditorium of the college. How that music moved me!

I had learned Cal liked music—played the piano. We spent an afternoon playing the piano. I think the room with the piano may have been in another dorm on campus.

One Sunday afternoon we rode the trolley to the end of the line and took a walk in a field. Cal was ingenious in finding inexpensive things for us to do. Neither a freshman college student nor an Army private had money to waste.

We attended church at the Presbyterian Church where we had met a time or two. He had not been shipped out when we had a dance at the gymnasium. How fortunate I felt to have an escort to invite! He did ship out soon after that. I had a letter or two from him after he left. I received a picture he sent of himself in Rome. Soon after he left, the war ended. Only this current year was I able to learn, after I found his name on the Internet, that he made it back home to use his streetcar token that he kept in his pocket to get home. And he is a professor of choral music. I blush to remember that I played the piano for Cal, who had been so kind. He seemed sweet and untouched. I feel privileged to have known that young man from Pennsylvania for a short time. We both seemed to enjoy the same things and loved God, but we did not talk about our faith.

One Sunday, we went uptown to attend the Baptist Church on Market Street. He wanted to show me a sign advertising Conshohocken Tires. Perhaps he wanted me to know how to spell it.

Eleanor Roosevelt visited Woman's College campus in the fall of 1944 that same school year. Sitting way up high in the auditorium, I could not hear what she said. Within the same school year, April 12, 1945, Franklin D. Roosevelt died. We were in the dining hall when it was announced that he had died in Warm Springs, Georgia. He was buried in Hyde Park, New York, April 15th. Many besides me felt sorry for Vice President Harry Truman, who succeeded him.

After I had a very poor start in chemistry, my teacher seemed as pleased as I when I received an acceptable first semester final grade. By the end of the spring semester, my grades improved more, and Alice Ryan, my chemistry teacher, suggested that I stay there and major in chemistry. By then, I knew I was heading to Carolina to become a pharmacist. I had learned that I would have had to go to North Carolina State to major in forestry. Nevertheless, I had come to love my freshman year, the campus of the school, and respected my instructors at Woman's College.

That summer at Hatteras, the young crowd spent a lot of time at the Bird Cage, going to the beach to swim, or just hanging around. Nothing was the same that summer of 1945. With the ending of the war, the service boys had moved on to other bases or been discharged from the service. Some of our girls had married or had moved away to work. At Hatteras, only Louise Oden, who attended Louisburg College, and I were college students at home for the summer. We had a pleasant vacation, dated some of the local fellows, but by fall I looked forward to learning what that elusive study called pharmacy had to offer me. And I had to wait until October to begin, because Carolina was still on the quarter system.

Chapter 18
My Quiet Years

❦

*E*xcept *for my head, I always had great health. You have heard that the weakest part of the body is one most subject to disease.* While I did not think of lazy eye or hearing loss as disease, I often made a sick joke, "From my head down, I'm in great shape!"

All my stories are about a teenage girl whose life was neither normal nor ordinary, because of my early hearing loss.

Hilda Ballance Brown had taught me in seventh grade. A great teacher, she made me conscious of the fact that others see the back of my neck, which I cannot see. I think she was looking at someone else's neck, but ever afterwards, I have been sure to wash my neck every day. She caught Keith Peele and me passing notes and embarrassed me by commenting, jokingly, "Love in the seventh grade!"

That year, 1939-40, I was the last one in the class to have measles and was very ill. I did not realize immediately that I had lost most of my hearing. My mother thought I had become an inattentive teenager. I thought others were leaving me out of conversations.

Sitting in dark, old wooden pews of Hatteras Methodist Church in 1943 for my baccalaureate service, I strained to hear our speaker and prayed for my ears to be opened. That summer, a local doctor used a painful procedure, in which he attempted with probes and wires up my nasal passage to sinuses and Eustachian tubes to clear away any obstructions and to equalize air pressure on both sides of the ear drum. He had no way of knowing if they were equal or not. His method failed.

Away at college in Greensboro, I consulted an ear specialist. Not very optimistic, he suggested removal of old tonsil tissue, left from the pre-school tonsillectomy required for school enrollment in 1932. Mine had been done with a bunch of other cousins in a clinic in Manteo, the Dare County seat of government.

So after school ended for the summer, my mother came by boat and bus, some hundred miles, to meet me in Washington, North Carolina. I had arrived the night before, checked into a hotel, and was scared all night after the young man at the desk had called my room to ask if I would like to come down and have a drink with him. Every sound outside my door that night put me on edge.

The operation proved futile. I did not know that immediately. Mama and I spent a day or two with one of her many nieces in Belhaven before we returned home after the operation. The crabmeat she served for dinner would have been wonderful had my throat not been so sore. It remained so for a long while.

Impaired hearing affected every part of my life. Social contacts were strained because I misunderstood. Asking over and over again, and being caught talking when a meeting had begun, embarrassed me. I faked a lot, tried to outguess the speaker, and joked about my mistakes.

Between 1940 and 1964, hearing impairment insulated me from many sounds I had once heard. Not until 1956, did I learn what had happened to my hearing and the name of the condition: Oto sclerosis is a condition in which bones of the inner ear fuse and cease to vibrate to transmit sounds from the ear drum to the auditory nerves connecting to the brain. Sometimes the loss is hereditary, and measles also can cause hearing loss.

I had graduated from the University of North Carolina School of Pharmacy in 1949 by persistence and good fortune. Sitting on front rows next to someone who took good notes was my good fortune. Charlotte Borders Plemmons gets credit for helping me graduate. Only in my final year did I acquire an inadequate hearing aid, which I quickly abandoned.

By 1956 Don, two sons and I were living at Hatteras. An aunt of mine brought me an issue of Look Magazine that told about a remarkable work of Dr. Samuel Rosen of New York. By stapes mobilization he reversed the effects of oto sclerosis. Case histories cited in the article sounded very like my own.

I wrote Dr. Rosen at once. Audiograms he recommended proved I might be helped by the operation. With a year in between the operations, Dr. Rosen did both ears, neither successfully. I had been so hopeful. I tried to convince myself that I did hear better than I had, but it was not true.

Dr. George Ferguson of McPherson Eye, Ear, Nose, and Throat Hospital in Durham, North Carolina, encouraged me to have the operation redone on the left ear in 1964. New advances made more positive results possible. The nerves in both ears were still functioning. While the right was still the best ear, we decided to do the left, which had distracting noises since my second operation and made hearing even harder.

When Dr. Ferguson operated, he found a shattered footplate and stapes hanging useless. He removed these. Into my ear, he explained, a small stainless steel piston now acted for them. I could hear, with no noises to interfere.

Work, schedules, deaths, living, and it was 1982 when an accident that punctured my left ear drum made me afraid. By then, Dr Ferguson had retired, and I contacted Dr. Carl Patterson, who treated my ear. My left eardrum healed, and my hearing in that ear had not been further impaired. However, fear of being plunged into quiet exile again made me decide I should have the operation on my right ear. Those results were better than expected.

I had missed my own baby's cooing but could now hear baby language other than angry crying. The results of these two ear operations made it possible for me to again hear the wind on my cheek, bird songs, and the sound grass makes as it is pulled from the ground. I felt like my whole body had been rewired, and I could hear my own body sounds again. I enjoyed conversations. I could hear airplanes overhead, trains in the distance, cars in the driveway and road, and the ring of the telephone without being a foot or two from it. A new world became mine, and my family, my friends, and I had to adjust to my hearing again.

Chapter 19
God in My Life

❧

From my mother I first learned the particulars of my birth on Hatteras Island. How Maurice Bernard Folb, Chief Pharmacist Mate at Cape Hatteras Naval Station, accepted the responsibility for delivering a ten-pound baby girl. Acting as doctor or obstetric nurse, he delivered many babies during a period when the Island was without a doctor.

Years later, "Doc" Folb told me he made those deliveries and gave other medical assistance to Island residents under the definition of "medical emergency." Naval regulations required he write up each of these as First Aid in his station's records. He told me something else that made me wonder. He said, "During your delivery, Sybil Dean, your mother prayed the most beautiful prayer I have ever heard."

All my life I have felt under the care and authority of God. My mother's prayer at my birth is, I believe, part of my spiritual heritage, which neither she nor I fully understood. The spiritual, "I Know God Has His Hand On Me," is significant to me in that I have felt all my life His call and the responsibility that goes with it.

Mama told me about Jesus when I was no more than four. More than anything, I identified with the rejection and suffering of Jesus' death. I hated the injustices and ignorance of those responsible for his passion and crucifixion.

When I was christened as a baby, I became enrolled as a preparatory member in Hatteras Methodist Church. I loved that old church and all its activities, as well as those of our school. I mouthed the words that Jesus loved me and suppose for a while I did believe it. However, there came a time around pre-adolescence when I no longer took His love for granted and thought I needed to be deserving.

I wanted to be like Jesus. I wanted the assurance of His favor. I remember being deeply moved by a movie, "Sign of the Cross," when I was very young. The story of the early persecution of Christians made me wonder if I could be faithful under the threat of death or punishment.

Because I believed in God's authority, I expected life to be fair. However, I found that life is not fair. I wanted to be right with God and thought others felt the same. By disappointments and misunderstandings, I learned the truth. Goals and ideals people hold vary greatly. Not all are intent on obeying God. Nor do they want to learn from Him. They know the Ten Commandments, and I suppose all believe they should obey them. Understanding is different from one person to the next. It was in the village where I lived then. It is now! However, the fact that we had no jail and no police seems to indicate they had a marked influence on the life of the community.

Evangelistic services during my childhood lasted for two weeks, becoming more and more intense each evening. Fear of fire and brimstone was reason enough to get right with God and took me to the altar under a man named Trueblood. I felt convicted and repented of my sin so I would not go to hell.

When I was twelve years of age I joined the church. However, it was many years before I understood the grace of God in the death and resurrection of Jesus Christ, which had freed me the moment I believed. Reflecting on the story of John Wesley, the founder of the Methodist Church, I learned that he too went through a long period of trying to win God's favor before he understood the truth of God's unconditional love and acceptance.

The loyalties of my father's parents had been to the Northern Church. As long as they lived, Uncle Deck and Aunt Alice Oden remained faithful in leadership to that church of diminishing membership and interest. Until the Episcopal (Northern) Methodist Church washed off its blocks, and the bishops decided to be done with the animosities of the Civil War and have only one Methodist Church, we attended both. Mama took us up the road to church in the morning and to Sunday school at the church down the road in the afternoon.

As a result of the 1939 merger, three Methodist bodies (Methodist Episcopal, Methodist Episcopal South, and Methodist Protestant) became one church. So the church down the road closed. Village people hated losing their church. Few felt comfortable going to the church up the road. So, when the Pentecostal Movement made a neutral church available, most of those people transferred their loyalties to the Pentecostals.

Some in derision called them Holy Rollers. Curiosity took us children down the road on Sunday afternoons to see for ourselves. They had a fervor that we liked. The music was lively, and they did indeed fall in the floor and sometimes shouted. In the beginning, they met in an old house, located about where Lee Robinson once had a store and where Virgil Willis now has a business. The site of the tent where we attended as teenagers seems to have been where the Assembly of God Church now stands.

As a teenager, I pumped and played the old organ for singing during our Methodist Youth Fellowship meetings. After Methodist Youth Fellowship some Sunday evenings, a bunch of us would go down to the tent to hear Alice Jeannette, a lady preacher from Buxton. She would get emotional about the lost. You could hear the tears in her voice. Some shouted, talked in tongues (glossolalia), and they sang with more joy than we had ever experienced in church. My heart heard.

Reading the Bible for myself, I learned that what was happening in Hatteras and Buxton with the Pentecostals had been usual for the early church after the death of Christ. Brother Shank told me that Grandma Mogie used to shout in the Methodist Church. It is historically true that the Holiness movement came out of the Methodist Church. I began to suspect the scornful criticisms were wrong, theologically and morally.

Pentecostals were very strict in the beginning. The women wore no makeup and wore their hair in the old style, straight with a knot at the back of their heads. They did not attend movies or dances and shunned adornment. Their discipline caused confusion in my life. I wanted to be right with God, yet I loved to dance and did not quite believe helping nature by a bit of color to my face would keep me out of heaven.

I tried to formulate ideas about God by reading the Bible and incorporating what others said to help me decide how God wanted me to behave. I sublimated my feelings and exaggerated my expectations for myself and for others. I became disappointed with myself and disillusioned with friends when our responses and actions fell short. Joyless, full of guilt, unsure of my worth, I sometimes filled up with self-hate and disgust. Besides the emotional battle, my hearing impairment often caused me to feel left out of conversations and tense from attempting to understand and respond appropriately. No one knew my dilemma except God and me.

As a child in Hatteras I was always trying to be good enough to be accepted by God. I did not understand how He had provided for my forgiveness by the death of His Son. I lived by the law instead of by the gospel message of atoning grace. I tried hard to be good and monitored my behavior by what I understood to be the way Jesus would live. My behavior was not gross. However, I lacked peace and joy. Being good could not give these to me.

As an older, avid reader, I read religious books, studied the Bible, and psychology and embraced Dr. Norman Vincent Peale's "The

Power of Positive Thinking." I listened to Billy Graham and other radio pastors. I taught a church school class, sang in the choir, served as a church leader, joined a prayer group, always searching for the reality I heard others talk about. I sought Christian fellowship with the fervor of a sports fan.

Home alone one morning, after my husband had left for his classes at the University of North Carolina and my sons had left for school, I had an experience with God for which I had longed all my life. Reading a familiar Scripture in my Bible, I suddenly felt it become alive and fresh. I realized I could choose to believe. At last, I knew I did not have to be perfect, nor have scientific proof to believe—only faith. God gives each person a measure of faith, but believing is a choice each must make for oneself.

God met me where I was. I do not remember which Scripture I read that day. More important, the Holy Spirit witnessed to my spirit and I cried from the very depth of my soul, "Abba, Abba, it is so simple. How could I have missed it when I have been searching so long?"

Tears flooded my eyes and wet my face. At last I did understand God's grace. Guilt and shame lifted from my spirit. God loved me! My unreliable opinion of my performance and myself was changed by God's forgiveness. I knew God for the first time as my ally instead of my judge. At last, I claimed the freedom in Christ Paul so often wrote about, no longer trusting my own goodness and behavior. At last I was free to accept myself, relying on Christ's righteousness, not on my virtue.

Finding how wrong I had been was painful and humbling, but freeing. Walking in faith, I began to examine old beliefs.

During a crisis in my marriage, I became convinced that God had to be first in my life. I could live without my husband, but I could not live without God. When the choice concerned a very precious human relationship, God asked Abraham to choose. Like Abraham, I knew I must decide whether to believe and obey God or my own insecure emotions. God was faithful. Having chosen God to be first in my life,

I did not have to make the human sacrifice I imagined I had to make. Instead, the relationship with my husband began to change subtly. It became better.

My new freedom in Jesus redefined my life as a daughter and mother. I had a new perspective. Fears and guilt no longer taunted me. The revelation of truth had shown me that I must let my spouse and my sons accept the responsibility for their lives. Their failures were not my fault. God was and is the authority for my life. My responsibility became to love, looking to God for wisdom to know how to love those important people and all others in my life. My life's quest has been for the Truth. God is Truth. Now I know that God's grace and presence were always mine, a treasure locked behind disbelief. Yes, God loves even me!

Chapter 20
My Mother's Hands

❧

I see my mother's fine-boned, capable hands sewing on buttons, making a patch, hemming a skirt, piecing and quilting bright quilt tops, sewing doll clothes to dress all our dolls for Christmas.

I see them, dripping wet with meal and water, shape and pat gray dumplings that she drops into a bubbly pot of collards with potatoes and a wedge of salt pork—her favorite meal.

I see them wilted in the soapy wash and the blue rinse water, as she washes clothes for a big family and boarders. Wringing the big white sheets and bulky work pants, sometimes using an elbow too, she uses one small hand to find a small piece, a handkerchief, and she squeezes it almost dry.

In the sunshine and breeze I see her nimble fingers arrange the pieces for hanging and pin them to the white clotheslines; see her take the dry, sweet-smelling clothes from the lines to fold into neat piles in a wicker basket to be ironed—with her hand curled around the handle of a heavy flat iron—later an electric one—to make them wrinkle free. I see her packing them away in the big oak ship drawers used for linens and in bureau drawers of five children and one spouse.

As her own accompanist, her short fingers straining for an octave, she moves her hands across the piano keys to make music as she sings of her faith.

Holding a book, she reads "The Elephant Child" by Rudyard Kipling, with delightful imitations of that foolish elephant. Pinching her nose between finger and thumb as the crocodile pulls and pulls an elephant nose into a trunk, she intones, "Plez let go my no'e!"

I feel her arms around me as she rocks me on her lap and sings my favorite song, "Now, honey, you stay in your own back yard. Don't mind what de white chile do. What do you 'spose dey's goin to give to a little black coon like you? Jest stay on yo side of the high boa'd fence and, honey, don't cry so hard. You may go out and play jest as long as ya' please, but stay in yore own back yard."

My heart breaks for that "poor lonesome little coon." Her hands comfort and soothe me as she wipes away my tears.

I see her pale, freckled hand curled around a baby chick wrapped in a rag, or a little white puppy. I see her tuck the sick animal inside her dress front, between her soft, full breasts, for healing warmth.

I feel her hands as she ministers to me when I have measles; see her fold the wet washcloth she puts over my burning eyes; hear the movement of the bedclothes as she lifts, straightens, and tucks them comfortingly close to my body with loving hands.

On her knees, her hands covered with fine peppery sand, she holds a cutting and buries it deep into the damp dirt, letting it rest on its side to grow roots.

Shovel in her hands, she digs another hole, while covering the last one, in which to bury more trash to build up the low places in the yard. Recycling, composting, reusing everything. Long before the age of recycling, she saves, conserves, preserves, and teaches her children to be accountable to and for the earth.

I see her hand with the plain gold band, her only jewelry, move nervously as she teaches a church school class of intermediates, and I wonder if she is nervous.

Her wet soapy hand shows me, a new mother, how to bathe a new first child more easily, and quickly to diaper and dress him. I see her knowing hands hold my clean, sweet infant close to her heart.

I see her slender fingers lift the Scrabble tiles to place them on the table before her to begin her favorite game.

Wasted by illness, her hands, now quiet, rest on the white hospital covers. Cancer and narcotics have taken vitality from them. I see them cold and lifeless, stilled by death.

I imagine our Savior taking both of those soft, warm hands into his own nail-scarred ones, looking into her blue dancing eyes, beneath shining, auburn hair, saying, "Well done, Inez, thou good and faithful servant; thou has been faithful over a few things, I will make thee ruler over many things: enter thou into the joy of thy lord." Matthew 25:21 (KJV)

Inez Lynn Daniels Austin
March 3, 1890—March 23, 1969

Chapter 21
Adonis Appears

❧

*D*estiny brought me to the University of North Carolina Pharmacy School at Chapel Hill in October of 1945. The man I met and eventually married arrived one week after his discharge from the United States Coast Guard, at the conclusion of World War II.

Orientation and registration over, classes began. Standing in line at Lenior Dining Hall that first morning, I heard one of the fellows behind me say, "My first class is in Phillips Hall."

"Mine too!" I said as I turned.

The speaker, the most handsome man I had ever seen, towered above me. His six-foot-tall slender frame dwarfed my five-foot-two one. I had to lift my brown eyes to meet his hazel, yellow-flecked ones. He had sun-bleached blond hair and a beautiful, clear, sunburned complexion. His friendly smile and pleasant northern accent entranced me.

Leaving the dining hall, I took a wrong turn. I still cannot read maps well. I arrived late to my mathematics class. When I walked into the assigned room, an arm clad in the red and black Worcester Academy athletic jacket shot into the air. There he was again. When the class was split, I ended up in the same class, the only female, with him and other veterans, whom I came to know. I looked for that jacket he wore in every crowd, searching for the man I had begun to dream about, whether awake or asleep.

In the months ahead we ate breakfast together, due to our schedules more than by intention. We were on the quarter system and had that eight o'clock math class five days a week. I learned he was a tennis player. He had come, under the GI Bill of Rights, from Massachusetts to have a longer tennis season and to play tennis for John Kenfield, the Carolina Varsity Coach.

When McIver Dorm had its first dorm dance, I invited him and some of his friends. Each girl had four or five cards to give to young men on campus. I bought a black net formal with a single ruffled shoulder strap and a big sweetheart red rose at the waist, for the sole purpose of impressing this blond god.

He complimented me when we danced and promised to ask me to one of the dances on campus. I was devastated when he invited a pharmacy classmate of mine to go as his date to the first scheduled dance. I persuaded my date to take me to that dance at Woollen Gymnasium. When my dreamboat broke on my partner, I began to tremble within the circle of his arms.

"You're trembling," he said.

Embarrassed and helpless, I said, laughing, "You do this to me." I lied. I was furious that he had invited that other girl after he had promised to ask me.

We still ate breakfast together and had the same class, but I began seeing him on campus with another girl regularly and began to despair. One day before Christmas holidays, he walked me from the math class to my dorm "to discuss mathematical problems," he said. While we talked in the parlor of my dorm, he showed me his draft card with his address, and I remembered so I could send him a Christmas card, which really surprised him.

On my birthday in January, I walked past his dorm, beyond mine, on my way to my noon gym class. He and another fellow were on the bank across from his dorm tossing a football. He called to me and asked if I would like to go to a movie with him that evening. What a nice twentieth birthday gift! I almost skipped and wanted to shout the rest of the way.

After that date, we became steadies. He taught me all about sports, which had not been part of my rural, fishing village background, but very important to his urban, prep school one. I took tennis in gym class with the purpose of learning to keep score, for when I first watched him play on the Varsity Tennis Team I had him losing the match instead of winning it.

Chapter 22
Cultures Clash

❦

Daddy had begun renovating the house, throwing the old roof out the attic windows, after a wider, longer roof had been constructed above it. The floor above the store, where our bedrooms should have been, was open space. Beds were sitting in the middle of the floor. We were definitely not ready for a visitor. I had not known how to dissuade him from coming. My gentle hints had not deterred him, and before he returned to his family in Waltham, Massachusetts, Don Skakle came to Hatteras to see me.

Years after, Don enjoyed telling the story of his trip over the sand and about the bus driver's reaction when he had told him he planned to visit the Austins at Hatteras. "Austins? Which Austin?"

"The one who has a daughter named Sybil." No problem there, because everyone knew everyone else in Hatteras village. The driver knew me.

When he arrived at Hatteras for the first time, having taken the Midgett Brothers Bus, built onto a truck body, over the sand and twisting ruts, I was at my brother's home with a bunch of young people, including my date. When Mama came to the front door in her housecoat, my first thought was that something had happened to Daddy. She called, "Sybil, there is someone here to see you."

My feelings were ambivalent when I saw him. I had tried to discourage him from coming. Had I realized the imposition his visit would be, perhaps I could have been more emphatic, if that were possible for the person I was at that time in my life.

He had first made a visit to Sparta, North Carolina, to see a girl he had dated at Carolina before me. She had dropped out of school at the end of the first semester. It was then Don and I began to date. Had he told me he was going there after school's end, I would have definitely told him not to show up at my door.

As it was, I felt torn between family and him the whole week. It was expediency that had us spend the first night with Ruby and Shank, my only brother. The next day a bedroom at the front of my parental home upstairs was enclosed and could give our guest privacy. My bed was in an open part of the hall. The bathroom still had walls, and Mama and Daddy's bedroom, at the back of the hall, beyond where I slept, had been completed. When Don stopped by my bed to plant a kiss on my cheek on his way to the bathroom, I was startled and afraid Mama and Daddy would hear him and misunderstand.

Even worse were our living quarters in the other part of the house. Part of the floor was missing. My guest seemed oblivious to it all.

I took Don to the Beacon, the gathering place for the young people of the Island, expecting him to enjoy it as much as I did. He did not appreciate it. He did not understand. A city boy, he had different expectations, different experiences. He expressed criticism of my parent's wisdom in letting me go and of my desire to be there. Our dancing, to the jukebox, kept the night from being a complete disaster.

Walking home from the Beacon that night, we paused on the Slash Bridge. I had told him it was the most romantic spot in Hatteras. But the moon was not shining on the Slash surface that night. Attempting to make it romantic, he said, "I wish I could ask you to marry me."

"I wish you could," I replied, but my heart was not in agreement.

He had hitchhiked to western North Carolina and back to Manteo.

By the time he arrived at Hatteras, Don had no money. Credit cards were unknown. He had no reserves. His G I Bill stipend had been exhausted. When it came time for him to leave, we put him on Daddy's freight boat going to Elizabeth City, and Mama gave him enough money for his bus ticket to Waltham, Massachusetts. A protective mother, she objected to his thumbing. For her, it was the simplest solution. She must have been as relieved as I was to see him go. I was glad to be home with my own kind.

Adonis did not seem the god he had been at Carolina. There, we sought like goals and associated with those seeking similar ones. He was admired as a member of the Carolina Varsity Tennis Team. At Hatteras, where my friends knew little about tennis or the expectations of the college crowd, he did not fit.

Chapter 23
Conflict and Resolution

❧

We wrote letters back and forth faithfully all summer. While he took part in tennis tournaments in New England, he drew money from the U. S. Government from the fund that paid returning servicemen—fifty-two weeks, I believe it was—while they decided what they would do with the rest of their lives.

The evening Don arrived, another former Coast Guardsman, a village man doing the same thing, had been in the crowd at Shank and Ruby's home. One night after Don had gone, he asked if he could drive me home. I was spending the night with Marian. Her father, Mr. Dolph, had sold the house he had built in Buxton and had bought the Dozier Burrus home from Mr. Dozier's youngest son, Maurice Burrus. Maurice had acquired the Dr. Kenfield home behind the Hatteras Methodist Parsonage. So, we got a drive home that night instead of having to walk home through the sand.

Marian went inside. We sat talking in his car for a while. I confessed to him that large crush on him when we were very young. He is the one who got his typhoid shot just before I did in 1936. He confessed that he had been interested in me, but a little afraid of me, too. I understood. My cousin Ruby, six months older than I, had advised that the way to interest a fellow was to "treat them mean and make them like it." I guess I overdid it. My slights and sarcasm had not had the effects I hoped. Now I learned what their effect had been.

We had been unlearned puppies. Puppies growl and bite as they tumble in play, acting fierce. Now that latent puppy love presented a problem to me. I found myself very attracted to this dark-haired, blue-eyed man that I thought looked a lot like Clark Gable. That swagger of his...!

He asked, "Why don't you be my girl?"

He had met Don that night he came. I told him that we expected to marry some day. "It's too late," I said and we both admitted that our dating would be unfair.

During our conversation, he had told me of seeing George overseas. We had much catching up to do. In spite of our resolve, we dated that summer, and when the summer ended, I was unsure about my feelings.

"I have to go back and see how I feel about Don," I told him.

"Sometimes I think I want to drag you off by the hair of the head like a caveman," he said laughingly.

"Sometime I wish you would," I said.

I did go back. I told Don about my confusion. It made him angry that I had dated someone else. My unexpressed feeling was: How do I know that you did not date someone too? After all, he did go to Sparta before he came to Hatteras.

That fall, his folks came to Chapel Hill to a ball game. They liked me. I liked them. When Don insisted he wanted me to come home with him for Christmas, his mother wrote my mother and father and asked that I be allowed to come. They agreed reluctantly.

We rode a Greyhound Bus all the way. This southern girl was going farther north than she had ever been. While we were there, they had a snowstorm. I had never seen so much snow. We walked on Beacon Hill to hear the carolers on Christmas Eve night. I cannot believe I did that in high-heeled, open-toed shoes. We never did find the carolers.

His brother Gordon, a discharged serviceman from the Navy who was recovering emotionally from a broken marriage that occurred during the war, was living, for the present, with their parents. He took us to see a hockey game in Boston Square Gardens. And another time we enjoyed the Ice Capades there with Don's mother and father.

Don took me to the places significant to his childhood and youth. To the hill where he and his friends had ridden a bobsled and to the pond where they ice-skated. Concerned about my hearing, he had his mother make an appointment for me to see their doctor for an opinion.

I ate winter squash for the first time and loved it. His mother's turkey did not cause "allergies," probably because there were no dark chocolates for me to eat besides. It was a wonderful visit. Everyone made over the southern girl Don had brought home for Christmas.

One night, his parents and Don took me next door to play billiards at Piety Corner Club. The four of us played bridge. New England and the Skakles were a delightful new experience for me.

After Christmas, due to the snow, we took a train from Waltham to Norfolk, and from there, a bus to get to Hatteras. While we were there, Don asked Daddy and Mama for their permission to marry me. Daddy agreed he would pay my tuition until I graduated. "Don't see any difference," he said, "in paying it with you married and paying it until she graduates and having you get married then."

Chapter 24
Getting from Chapel Hill
to Hillsborough in 1947

*E*ven while we asked permission, we were planning to marry *before September, and when we returned to Chapel Hill, we began to put our plan into practice.* If we had to have blood tests, I have forgotten. We did have to have a license. The county seat for Orange County is Hillsborough, only thirteen miles from Chapel Hill.

We decided we would marry on Valentine's Day, 1947. So, one Saturday morning we took a bus from the makeshift bus station in a paint store on Columbia Street, across from what was then Chapel Hill Town Hall. We boarded the Trailways red-and-cream-colored bus for Durham. The bus followed a twisting road for many miles more than it takes these days on the Chapel Hill-Durham Boulevard to a bus station in Durham. We had to take another bus to Hillsborough from Durham.

We arrived sometime before noon, and entered the Orange County Court House looking for the Registrar of Deeds office. We met a man in the hall who told us that the Court House was closed on Saturday. We had no feathers to fall, but we were a couple of sick, sad birds. I have no idea how much our adventure to obtain a marriage license cost us, or how many meals the sacrifice represented. We had saved our pennies from our meals and with those had bought two plain gold bands at Wentworth and Sloan on Franklin Street. Mine cost five dollars and his heavy one about four times as much.

This was a definite setback for two starry-eyed young folks, ignorant of the ways of governments unless it had already affected us in some way. Fortunately, the man we met and spoke to was the man we needed to see. We told him how we had arrived, and he took pity on us.

"I can give you the license," he said. He must have been the Registrar of Deeds for Orange County. And so he did, for whatever a marriage license cost in those days.

With the license in hand, we boarded a bus that would take us to Durham to catch another back to Chapel Hill and the University of North Carolina Campus in time for our meal at Lenior Hall, where I managed to eat for one dollar a day, and Don spent one dollar and a half and was forever hungry. My monthly stipend from home was forty dollars, and his, from the United States Government G. I Bill was sixty-five dollars. On Sunday, we splurged and ate our favorite meal at the Carolina Coffee Shop on Franklin Street: veal cutlets in tomato sauce with mashed potatoes and green beans. On Sunday, I spent a dollar-fifty to cover that meal.

Coming home on the bus, we had decided that since we had our license in hand, we would move our marriage date up a week. Yes, we were eager to be joined by marriage so we could enjoy a physical union. We had a lot of quick plans to make. We visited the Rev. Charles Jones at the Presbyterian Church, the same Charles Jones who was to become embroiled in the civil rights issue the following year, to ask him to marry us on a Friday afternoon. Don called the Robert E. Lee Hotel in downtown Winston Salem for reservations for two nights. We had a couple of married friends, Betty and Frank Zimmerman, in whom we confided. They were to be our witnesses. Somehow, our roommates discovered our plans, and Constance Smith and Robert Graham joined our wedding party.

All I could afford to buy for my wedding attire was a blue blouse at Berman's Department Store. I wore this with my black suit, hoping the old superstition expressed in the nursery rhyme would give the blue more influence.

"Marry in blue, your love will be true.

Marry in black, you'll wish yourself back."

February 7, 1947, dawned clear, sunny, and not too cold. Don had bought me a rose corsage. Someone took pictures of us on Hillsborough Street, outside McIver Dorm, and at the church. It is good they did, for that planned additional September ceremony never happened.

Colored film was new to amateur camera owners in 1947, and expensive. We were going to visit friends in Winston Salem. Someone spoke to us at the bus station and questioned the occasion of the flowers and trip. Our lies did not make us feel less guilty.

Honeymoon over, we came back to Chapel Hill on the bus to our respective dorms, where we would live until school ended in June. Our rash actions had left Don, especially, very short of cash. In order to make our funds stretch until the end of the month, we bought food at the grocery store and had picnics. Even Lenior's cheap fare was beyond our means. I would warm soup on the hot plate in the dorm laundry room and bring it down sometimes. No credit and no money made us very cautious and ingenious.

Our actions set in motion consequences, worries, and inconveniences. We became clandestine lovers, and I felt guilty. When I caught flu, I went to the infirmary, afraid that I was pregnant. Don came to see me faithfully. It took a week or two before food tasted good again.

We went home to Hatteras in March for spring break, wearing our wedding bands on chains around our necks. We took a Trailways Bus to Elizabeth City to get a free ride on my father's freight boat, Cathleen, to Hatteras. Uncle Horton, her captain, and his family were living in Elizabeth City. We went to visit as a good relative would. We had a hotel room, and no one knew we were married. When I told

Aunt Violet we planned to get married in September, she said, "How can you be so sure?"

How could I answer that one?

We got home and Don said, "Why don't we tell them?"

How I wish we had! It would have settled it then and there. I could not bring myself to confess our folly. So we slept in different rooms, except he would come to my room after the house settled down and leave before the house awakened next morning.

We came back by boat and bus to Durham and decided we would spend a night at the old Melbourne Hotel. When Don signed in, he forgot to sign us in as man and wife, and I blushed and sputtered. Living a lie was not much fun, even though we were passionately in love.

Planning ahead, Don thought we should buy a trailer. We would need a place to come back to after the ceremony in Hatteras in September. So we went to the trailer park on Columbia Street, where the Pharmacy School now is, to look over some trailers. We found one for five hundred dollars. We did not have any money, so we wrote and asked our parents. His folks came through with half of it. My parents refused. I have no idea what they thought.

So Don asked his tennis coach, John F. Kenfield, who went on a note with Don at The Chapel Hill Bank, for the money, to be paid out of the money Don made that summer working as assistant tennis professional at Lake Shore Country Club in Glencoe, Illinois.

I had lost credits transferring to Carolina from Woman's College of the University of North Carolina my sophomore year. I was to stay in summer school at Chapel Hill and catch up those credits. Don did not want to leave me at the University. Of course, I wanted to go to Glencoe instead of staying at Carolina in summer school. However, it meant we had to confess our deceit to our parents and friends. Our secret marriage had proved to be as complicated as our trip from Chapel Hill to Hillsborough to get our license had been. Like good parents, ours forgave us and continued to love and support us in countless ways.

We officially married in February, 1947, and spent our first summer in Glencoe, Illinois, where we worked at Lakeshore Country
Club, situated on Lake Michigan. He taught tennis for Coach
Kenfield, and I learned to cook hamburgers and make milkshakes
and "black cows" for the children of the membership, which included
Steins, Kuppenheimers, and Florsheims who visited the Cabana, situated by the swimming pool.

Our season ended in Glencoe, and we caught a ride with a fellow
who had worked there during the summer. He took us to Columbus,
Ohio. Don's mother and dad were visiting her mother, Clara
Edmunds, in Warren, Ohio, where Don had been born. They came to
Columbus to meet us and take us there.

We visited Grandma Edmunds and other relatives. They welcomed
me into the family and gave us gifts. On our way back to
Massachusetts, the senior Skakles took us to Niagara Falls before we
went to their home in Waltham, Massachusetts.

My life beyond the Outer Banks had truly begun. However, Don and
I were to make our home at Hatteras twice after our graduation from
Carolina in 1949 and 1950, once for the 1950-51 school year when Don
acted as principal of Hatteras School, and again between 1954-58 when
he managed and clerked in Austin's Store after his health demanded a
change of pace for him.

My life as Don Skakle's wife took me to interesting places, to envi-
ronments as unique as the Outer Banks, and to a life as challenging
as growing up there. As wife of a tennis coach and teacher, as mother of our three athletic sons, I had another sort of life. Donald
Edmund Skakle, Jr., was born at Duke Hospital, Durham, North
Carolina, in July, 1948, before either of us had graduated. Two other
sons graced our lives: Stanley Andrew, June 24, 1952, and Clifford
Dwight, October 26, 1956.

During the years between 1950 and his death in 1980, Don coached
many young men, who became part of our lives. He influenced others

whom he taught while on the physical education staffs of public schools and the University of North Carolina. Thus, I furthered my education in a direction very different. Maybe I will write the story of that passage someday, if I live long enough and God allows me eyes and hands to accomplish it. Here is a poem about my Adonis:

Adonis

"...Adonis was dearer to her than heaven." [15]

Once I met a man as beautiful as Lucifer.
His voice like music, his hair so fair—
His eyes ensnared my very soul.
Dazzled by his form, enticed by desire
In anguish I cried, "I want you more than God!"

—Sybil Austin Skakle

Footnotes

1. LAND GRANTS—Hatteras, Hatteras Banks, Vol-I 1735- 1764, (Grant #5048, pg 187) .

2. Ibid. (Grant #5596. p. 315).

3. Currituck Tax List, 1779, examined March, 1780, by Willis Ethereidge.

4. Affidavit in N. C. Genealogical Publication.

5. U. S. Census, 1790, Edenton District, Currituck County, Hatteras. (p. 20-22)

6. Inventory of estate Key commenced September term, 1777.

7. The second "l" is added to the spelling by 1877. "Stow" became "Stowe" later still.

8. Diary of John Rollinson.

9. Sally Anne married Charles Odin, the son of John, who is said to have washed ashore on a pork barrel after a wreck off Hatteras Island. According to one story, he washed ashore three times, first when a cabin boy. After the third time, John decided to stay, married Lovy Alice Stow, and became progenitor of a large family.

   Mogieannah Oden, born May 13, 1864, wife of William Wheeler, had three sisters. Sister Laura married Levin Quidley. They had three sons: Rueben, Norman, and Norris. Sister Victoria, nicknamed Puss, married Claughton Gray. Their children were: Rachel, who married Victor Balance, Harry, Charlie, Damon, Ralph, Harold, and Lennon, who had Downs Syndrome, which was shrouded in superstition and not understood even during my childhood.

   A third sister, born in 1868, had died in 1893. She had married Charles Peele, who moved his family away from Hatteras. I know little about that branch. Information compiled by The Historical Society of Hatteras Island will probably clarify and identify what happened to Peele and Lovie Alice Oden's children.

Brothers Singleton (Dock), Dexter (Deck), Andrew Shanklin and Moses Ransom chose wives and helped their sisters increase the population of Hatteras Village. Unfortunately, Ransom lost his wife and two daughters to tuberculosis, and his second marriage to Julia produced no heirs. Both Dock and Deck had large families, most of whom settled in Hatteras. Some younger sons of both Deck and Dock left the island to work on boats or join the U.S. Coast Guard and to establish families in other places.

The next generation of Oden (or Odin) and Austin broadened the boundaries of our family greatly. As I grew up and became interested in boys, I could hardly find a potential boyfriend not related to me through one family or the other. It was the nature of our isolation, surrounded on every side by bodies of water as we were, for cousins to sometimes marry.

Wheeler, my father's father, had one brother named Harmon (Harm). Their father had been married twice before he married their mother, Mathilda Styron. There was an Uncle Joseph who lived in Frisco, possibly Mathilda's son by her former marriage. One half-sister, Courtney, married William Gaskill.

Bill and Courtney Gaskill produced a large family of sons and daughters and kin folks with names of Stowe, Peele, Gaskill, and Ballance, while the Odens married Ballance, Midgette, Austin, Stowe, O'Neal, too many for me to identify.

Harmon married Betty Stowe and their offspring were sons: Perry, Crawford, and Lawrence; and two daughters: Blanche, who married Luther Dudley Burrus, and Delores (Lorie), who married Charlie Fulcher of Trent (Frisco). When I was a little girl, going visiting on a Sunday afternoon was pleasure for all of us. I remember Daddy taking us up to visit our Trent relatives and others.

10.   James Monroe, my father's oldest brother, born September 8, 1887, married Kate Stowe and fathered two daughters, Mogieannah (Brown) and Mary Harlow (Styron). He died January 22, 1956.

Daddy's birth, February 20, 1889, came next; and two years later Fred

Barrett, on February 22, 1891, joined the household.

Fred, married to Ruth Styron, owned the fish house. Their children were Frederick, Jr., Charlie Wood, Eliza (Robinson), Virginia (Coke), Velma (Gaskins), and Jessalyn (Walton). He died June 8, 1941 in Norfolk, Virginia, of a heart attack.

Lovie Alice, born August 19, 1893, married Elsworth Ballance. Their children were: Thurmond, Myrtis (Austin), Wheeler, and Gamaliel. Lovie, thirty-two, died of blood poisoning from a pimple on her face. Her youngest, Gamaliel was two years old at the time of her death, October 27, 1925.

Beatrice, born March 5, 1895, married Leo Peele. Names of their children follow: Juanita (Jennette), Leo Jr., Maxton, Nacie, Elise (Dixon), Beatrice (Barnette), Maurice, killed in a shooting accident, and Lovie Alice (Leatherwood). She lived to ninety, dying May 18, 1987.

Ernest, born February 13, 1898, married Decatur (Kate) Harrell, and acted as caretaker of Gooseville Gun Club. He died, October 14, 1931, of a brain tumor, leaving five children: Decatur (Tate), Minnie (Burrus), David, Avis (Davis), and Albert (Bert), two years old. Their oldest child, Desmond, died at thirteen of a ruptured appendix.

Nacie, born February 23, 1900, married Maude Peele, sister of Leo Peele, and they had two daughters, Ruby Erlene (Burrus) and Minerva (Johnson). He had a long productive life as a carpenter. He stepped off a scaffold on a building project and was paralyzed from the neck down for several years before his death January 18, 1969. Mama did a musical reading, "Crossing the Bar," at his funeral. She died March 23, 1969, of cancer, in Greenville, North Carolina.

Luther Lathan, born March 27, 1902, married one of Aunt Courtney Gaskill's granddaughters, Ellen Peele. Their children were Luther Latham, Jr. and Elizabeth "Libby" (Midgett). Luther worked as caretaker of Gooseville Gun Club for many years after Ernest died. When it no longer existed as a club, he did many jobs—fishing, carpentry, carving, and digging clams. He died April 10, 1986.

The youngest, William Horton, born August 23, 1907, married Violet Gaskill, a schoolteacher, from Wanchese. After his stint in the U.S. Coast Guard and as boat captain, he became a plumber and lived several years in Elizabeth City. He acted as funeral director for Hatteras Island for Twifords of Elizabeth City for many years after his return to the island and prior to his death, May 8, 1994. Their offspring are Patricia Jean (Burrus), Grady, and William Horton.

11. Three of Nancy's sons, George C., Tucker, and Crawford, lived in the home during Mama's early years. The oldest, George C., born 1874, died of a possible heat stroke April 19, 1893, at "19 years and 11 days." Mama, a tot then, used to speak of him and that tragic day when he came in from the field, lay down on the front porch and died. Did she remember, or only remember having heard her father or mother speak of the event? Papers concerned with her father obtaining the right to his belongings from the Life Saving Service are in the North Carolina Archives records, as well as the original handwritten will of George Charles himself. The younger George C. was supposedly home on leave when he died.

A year after the death of the first George C., George Columbus was born October 15, 1894. Geter Pritchard, born June 9, 1896, died March 16, 1897, the same year George Charles served in the North Carolina General Assembly as representative from Dare County. (Many Daniels before him and since my grandfather have served their state government and even today.)

Caswell (Cas) Hobson arrived September 11, 1898, and Tom Elden, September 12, 1902. Margaret was forty-two years old when her last child, Clarence Luther, was born October 9, 1904. She died nine years later, November 30, 1915.

George Columbus left home before his eighteenth birthday to join the Lighthouse Service. During World War I, he joined the Navy and served for the duration. After the war, he joined the Norfolk Fire Department. Soon he went to work for the Chesapeake Ferry Company, serving as captain on ferries from Willoughby Bay to Old Point Comfort, earning his masters license as a pilot on all oceans. He had remained in the United States Naval Reserve and served in active duty during World War II, attaining the rank of Commander. His job was to place and maintain nets in the area of Norfolk Naval Base and Norfolk Harbor to protect them from submarines and mines.

When the war was over, George joined the Virginia Ferry Company, as captain, running from Little Creek to the Eastern Shore. He was elevated to Port Captain and served in that capacity until his retirement.

He married Elsie I. White. They had one child, Virginia (Simmons). George remarried a few years after Elsie's death and died March 16, 1977, leaving behind many with whom he worked in Norfolk environs who loved and respected him. A lifetime member of Park Place Methodist Church of Norfolk, active in the Masons, he helped many of his kin and other young men to obtain licenses to work on ships. His gardening reflected his North Carolina beginnings.

Caswell also left home at a very early age. He went to Seattle, Washington, married Freda Uhrich, had a family of four, and could never afford to come east, even for his father's funeral, August 24, 1938.

During the depression years he had worked at anything he could to provide for his family. Primarily, he painted houses. Later, he joined the United States Geodetic Survey, which charted western coastal waters. A few years after Luther's discharge from the U. S. Coast Guard, he joined Cas. Both brothers retired from U. S. Geodetic Survey from Seattle, Washington.

It was Luther who first brought the three older children, Barbara, Tom and Dick, across country with him to visit kinfolk. Marge missed that trip. All four children were grown and married before Uncle Cas came back to Roanoke Island, land of his birth.

I only knew Tom from what Mama said about him and his picture of a smiling man with red hair. Like her, Tom loved music. They had enjoyed singing together around the pump organ in their home. He died in Scotland Neck, North Carolina—a young man of thirty—October 6, 1932. Proud of his physical strength, a clerk in a store, it was supposed that he overtaxed his heart by lifting loads too great. He left a two-year-old red-haired daughter named Betty Jo, Mona's age, and his young widow, Mattie Spears.

In 1976 Sister Marjorie and I visited Uncle Cas and wife Freda in Kirkland, Washington, meeting them for the first time. We also visited Uncle Luther and his second wife, Lucy Peele Peele of Hatteras, in Seattle. Lucy, a young widow with one daughter, Millicent, married Luther around 1947. Luther's first marriage to a Wanchese girl, Margaret Tillett, had ended in divorce. There were no children from either marriage.

Luther had lost a lung to cancer years before his death. When Sister Margie and I flew out to Seattle in 1976, we were going to say our good byes to him. He was taking oral doses of a very potent chemical, 5-Florouracil, the drug of choice then and before the discovery of more sophisticated chemotherapy. We believe he experienced a miracle of healing in answer to many prayers in his behalf. He lived ten more years, dying May 4, 1986. Neither he nor his wife Lucy or anyone else expected that Lucy would die of cancer before him.

12. When Lillian's widowed daughter Myrtle Tillett realized her mother was under too much stress for her health and age, she became caregiver for Aunt Rado. Stopping by unexpectedly one day, I found Aunt Rado lying contentedly in bed, smiling, smelling of Wind Song Cologne with a pink bow in her hair.

Elrado and her niece Myrt had a special bond of affection and understanding. Neither had grown up with their fathers. Elrado died in Elizabeth City hospital in her ninety-ninth year. She had hoped that the pacemaker put in place the year before would enable her to reach one hundred, which she so wanted to do.

Lillian married a Wanchese man, Nathan Daniels, a fisherman. He loved and served her until his death. They had no children. She sewed and waited on trade in their little store in Wanchese. They eked out a living.

13. Reference information used can be found in an article "New Deal," Microsoft (R) Encarta 97 Encyclopedia (c) 1993-1996. Microsoft Corporation, and "U.S. Depressions and Prosperity Since 1790," pgs 126-127, *The World Book Encyclopedia*, (c) 1960. Oral history provided by Hatteras natives, Mildred Stowe Willis and Herbert Oden for verification of names and circumstances. My sisters, Jo Oden and Ramona Hunter, helped.

14. *Hatteras Monitor*, August, 1993 (p.2).

15. Gayley, Charles Mills, *Classic Myths in English Literature and in Art*, based on Bullfinches "Age of Fable" (1855), Ginn and Co., Boston, Massachusetts, 1939, p. 126.